MW00936001

Four Shots in

the Dark

Jameson Kars

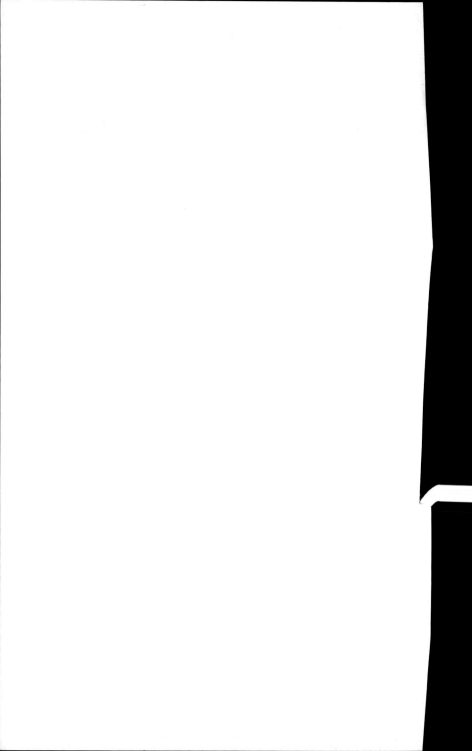

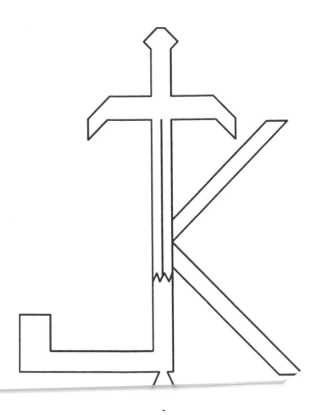

Chapter 1

"Forty five minutes late. You're forty-fucking-five minutes late. Do you really think I have time to sit around and wait for you all fucking day?"

The man sat at the counter of a small diner, his face twisted in rage and his cheeks a luminous hue of scarlet, spitting with every obscenity he barked as I approached. He barely managed to stay buttoned over his large stomach – with a tie. His dark brown hair was balding, so much so that the top of his head was covered with only a few thin strands of hair. If he had any dignity at all, he would have just shaved his head. It was not that his entire body lacked hair, though. As a matter of fact, what hair he lost on his head seemed to have reappeared on other parts of his body in twofold, sometimes even threefold, quantities. Tufts of hair peaked through the collar of the shirt he wore, something that would induce gagging amongst those who were so unfortunate to glimpse the sight. As if that were not enough, the armpits of his shirts were covered in such large sweat stains that he was sure to draw the stares of pedestrians on the sidewalk.

"Yet you're still here," I replied, taking a seat at the counter next to him.

"Only because I want to get this done. I am a very busy man."

"*Clearly*, your time cannot be that valuable if you were able to sit around and wait for forty-five minutes."

He was my antithesis. I wore a neatly pressed suit with a vibrant red tie. My blonde hair was slicked back and my pearly white smile caused the waitress to blush as she brought me a cup of coffee.

Sensing that my retort would not get a reply, I lowered my voice and continued the conversation. "Have you brought everything I asked for, Mr. Sanders?"

"Mr. Sanders? That's not my name," he said, a look of confusion on his face.

"My mistake. You just look so much like Colonel Sanders that I thought you must be a descendant. And the relation to a fried chicken mogul would explain what's going on down here," I finished, patting his stomach.

2

"Get off me," the balding man said, pushing my arm away. He reached into the jacket that hung on the back of the chair behind him, removed a small manila folder, and handed it to me. "Here's everything you asked for."

I perused the file. Everything seemed to be in order, so I closed it and turned back to the amorphous blob of human flesh.

"I have to run now," the balding man said. I wanted to chide that any amount of physical exertion would surely earn him a one-way ticket to the morgue, but he still had something I desired and I may have already reached my limit pushing his buttons.

"Not so fast. I believe you forgot something else."

The balding man reached into his jacket once more and pulled out a thickly stuffed envelope.

"There it is," I said, taking the envelope and putting it into my pocket.

"Aren't you going to count it to make sure it's all there?"

I believe that it's all there. We must maintain an appropriate level of trust, Mr. Sanders. That's the only way this relationship works." Now that I'd received what I wanted, I didn't feel the need to hold back any longer.

"God damn it, I told you that's not my fucking name," the balding man said, his annoyance quickly turning to disdain.

I could see the rage returning as his cheeks deepened to a reddish-purple color that I didn't know existed organically, unless you consider Barney organic, in which case there's no helping you. "I know that, but I do not remember your name, nor do I care to, so that's what I'm going to call you."

The balding man stood up and began to walk to the door without saying another word, but turned around before he got more than two steps away. "Can I ask you a question?"

"I wouldn't want to take up any more of your precious time than I already have." Sarcasm dripped from my lips like a leaky faucet.

"Shut the fuck up."

"You ought to be a little nicer, you know. After all, I'm the one doing you the favor."

"Then do me one more little favor and tell me how long it will take."

"It depends when the opportunity is right, but it will happen within the next forty-eight hours."

"Okay," the balding man replied, then walked out the door.

I looked around the restaurant. I was one of only four customers in the whole place. Granted, it was a small restaurant, but there were still more than thirty open seats. The other patrons all seemed to be immersed in one way or another and did not pay me any attention. Good. I didn't want to draw any suspicion. Not that anyone would have

4

known the nature of the meeting. I was always careful not to say too much, just in case someone was eavesdropping. Determining that it was safe, I decided to stay and finish my coffee.

A few minutes later, the waitress walked by. She smiled as she approached. Her blouse was unbuttoned further than when she brought my first cup of coffee. "He didn't finish his food," I said, pointing to the plate the balding man left behind. "Must have been trying to watch his weight."

"I hear avoiding broccoli is the way to do that," she said, pouring the untouched vegetables into the garbage in front of her, "especially on your third plate of the day."

"That was his third plate?" I grinned and shook my head in disbelief.

"In his defense, he was waiting for a while."

"It was only forty-five minutes! How does someone eat three meals in that amount of time?"

"I'd be impressed if I wasn't so disgusted. Each of those was twelve ounces of meat."

"He's the reason people go hungry."

"Imagine if he would have eaten only one meal," the waitress said, "then he could have given the other two away and fed a family of four!"

We both laughed, then looked at one another and smiled.

"What are you doing tonight?" the waitress asked. I was in.

"I'm busy tonight. But I have a few minutes right now." Dating wasn't really my thing. I was more interested in the part that came after.

"Oh yeah?" the waitress said, playfully daring me to finish my thought.

Before I knew it, we were in the bathroom having our own fifteen minute break. This had turned into a better meeting than I ever could have imagined.

After my little sexcapade with the waitress in the bathroom, I walked back to my apartment. I looked at the unopened mail that sat on the counter in the kitchen. Each piece of mail was addressed to Samuel Alterson. That was my most common alias, the one I used for people who I may have to interact with regularly. My real name was Julian Donahue, but no one knew that. I had no friends or family, except for a sister who I hardly ever talked to. The waitress got a different name, one that would lead nowhere. If I wanted another round with her, then I would walk down to the restaurant and tell her. She wouldn't object. They never did.

I threw everything besides the bills in the garbage, then walked into my office. I pulled out the manila folder that Mr. Sanders gave me and filed it away with dozens of other similar folders. After that, I took the money out of the envelope and put it in a small safe that masqueraded as a microwave. I ended the day the only way I knew how: drinking beer and watching a football game.

Chapter 2

A week later, it was time for me to make my monthly visit to the post office. I'd set up a P.O. box for anything pertaining to my real identity. Try as I might to get rid of it, there was still a paper trail connected to the name. I'd taken every precaution I could to ensure that my identity stayed hidden, even switching post offices each year so that I didn't visit the same place too many times.

The most recent post office I'd chosen was located just before the business district. Just beyond it, massive corporations loomed in the distance. Inexplicably, this part of Florida had become a hub for massive conglomerates and corporations. In the distance, the buildings for several prominent businesses could be seen. There was Polarized, a financial company; Vindicta, a company that easily had the largest building, though I wasn't exactly sure what the hell they did; and Green Leaf, the headquarters of an industrial company. If I continued past the post office, I would have come across more businesses, but it was rare that I ventured that far.

As I walked, I got the strange sensation that I was being followed. Stubborn and defiant by nature, being followed was something I didn't take too kindly. The last thing I needed was someone following me around and sniffing around my business. I valued privacy to the point of complete secrecy.

In an effort to shake my pursuer, I made two abrupt turns, but I could still feel the assailant behind me. I didn't slow down long enough to look over my shoulder, so the son of a bitch couldn't get any closer to me than he already was. Instead, I picked up my pace. Still, I continued to feel like I was being followed. The footsteps quickly turned into loud thuds and I was almost certain that I heard heavy breathing. I continued to the end of the block, then cut down an alley. Beads of sweat dripped down my forehead as I sped up again. I was so focused on evading the person behind me that I didn't notice a large fence until it was only a few feet in front of me. Out of options, I tried to climb the fence, but I was unsuccessful. It was simply too high to be scaled. With nothing else to do, I confidently turned to face my pursuer, and as I did so I let out a loud laugh.

"It's just you," I said, recognizing the balding man that I met with the previous week.

"Why'd – you – have – to – walk – so – fast?" he said, gasping for air between each word. "Now – I'm – all – sweaty."

"Don't give me that shit. You were probably sweaty way before you started following me. Speaking of that, why are you following me, anyway?"

"It's been a week," the balding man said, finally catching his breath, "and you still haven't done it."

"Ah, you see, that's the thing," I replied. "I'm not going to do it. I was never going to do it."

"What do you mean you're not going to do it?"

"That seemed like a pretty straightforward response to me. Let me try it again a little slower. I – am – not – going – to – do – it," I said, pausing between each word to nail home my point, though I realized it made me sound as out of breath as that fat fucker.

"I understood what you said. What I don't understand is why you're not going to do it. I did everything you said, gave you all the necessary information, and paid you half the money up front."

"Oh yes, I'm very aware of that, but that doesn't change anything. I'm still not going to do it."

"Well then I want my money back. If you're not going to finish the job, then you should at least return my money. It's only fair."

"That would be fair, you're right. But you're also operating under the assumption that I am a fair man, when, in fact, the opposite is true."

The balding man was at a loss for words. He could not believe my betrayal. Despite the fact that he didn't know me in the slightest, he never expected me to double-cross him. They never did.

"I can't fucking believe it. I just can't fucking believe it. Fuck. I'll...I'll...I'm going to..."

"You'll what?" I taunted. " Hurt me? Embarrass me? Ruin my credibility? *Kill* me?" I snickered. "You can't. You can't do any of that. You can't do anything. You gave me that file. All those pictures came from your collection. The handwriting is all yours. She'll recognize it. You even had the audacity to give me ideas of how I should do it! You planned everything and I have all the evidence. I don't think your wife would be very pleased to know that you hired me to kill her."

Chapter 3

A few days later, two men sat at a bar, drinking away another difficult week. One of the men was short with buzzed hair and an earring in his left ear. I'd later come to find out his name was Jordan Alticott. The other man, a Hispanic with spiked hair, was missing a tooth on the bottom of his mouth. His name was Carlos Padilla. Both men bore tell-tale signs of being blue collar workers. Their hands, legs, and arms were dirty. And, though each of them had changed clothes after getting off, both men wore heavily worn work boots.

Normally, I wouldn't be caught dead near a blue collar worker, but that was the nature of the bar. It served as the perfect location for men of means to discuss business without being overheard, but it also attracted lowlifes who couldn't have afforded my apartment's monthly rent payment with a year's salary.

I was on a scouting mission, so I wasn't dressed in my usual attire of a freshly pressed suit and slicked back hair. Instead, I wore khaki pants, a button up shirt with no tie, as well as a fake mustache and graying wig. It was imperative that I hid my identity, just in case things went south. So far, I'd been able to avoid any trouble, but you can never be too careful.

Not seeing any potential clients, I listened to the two converse.

Carlos spoke his broken English in such a thick accent that it took a trained ear, a Spanish-English dictionary, and a great deal of guesswork to comprehend the man. The dialogue hereafter is the best I could translate his mumbled blather.

"Did I ever tell you about the party that I threw in high school?" Jordan asked.

"I don't think you ever did, man," Carlos said. "Wait, was that when that girl tried telling you she was pregnant after she gave you a blowie?"

"No, that was a different story. But now that we're talking about that, I did end up fucking that girl a couple years later and that time she did get pregnant, but I convinced her that a different guy was the father. And she still believes it to this day, even though that guy's a nigger and the kid's whiter than a jizz-stained polar bear in a snowstorm."

"People like that shouldn't be allowed to have kids, you know? They should have some sort of test..." (indecipherable babbling) "... be a father. I know I wouldn't pass, but I don't think the world can handle another one of me running around," Carlos replied.

"Amen to that. But here's the best part of that story: the nigger thinks it's his kid too! They named him Damian Jr. or some shit. Whatever that guy's name was. Cuz you know niggers always name their kids after themselves."

"Fucking idiot!"

"I know. I have to tell you about that party, though."

Jordan stood up as he began his tale. Even with Carlos sitting on his barstool, Jordan's head still was shorter than Carlos's shoulder. Jordan was probably well into his thirties, but I assumed he got asked for his ID at every bar he went to. Not because he looked like he was under twenty-one, but because he was shorter than the average elementary school student. Tonight alone, the bartender had checked Jordan's ID three times, even after seeing the stamp on his hand, just to make sure that he hadn't switched places with a prepubescent teen.

"So, it all started when my parents went away for the week," Jordan began.

Carlos was on the edge of his seat, a shit-eating grin on his face. He was enthralled with his coworker. If that was someone he looked up to, it was time to get some new fucking idols.

"They decided to take a trip to Arkansas. Why the fuck they wanted to take a vacation to that shithole, I have no idea, but it was probably because they couldn't afford to go anywhere nicer.

"Anyway, they left me in charge of my two little sisters, and they gave me this whole speech about behaving myself and not having parties. All the usual parent bullshit. Honestly, I didn't even hear a word they said because I was planning the party as soon as they told me they were leaving for the weekend.

"So I invite about ten of my friends over and tell them to spread the word about the party. I'm expecting thirty, maybe forty people to show. Nope. Half of my class shows up. And I didn't go to one of those rinky-dink sheep-fucker-hick-town-nowhere schools. There must have been at least five hundred people there. And I was shitting my pants because my parents told me that all the neighbors were watching. There was no way they weren't going to notice five hundred people at my place. And even worse, the principal's two daughters showed up. They were two of the most straight-laced people I'd ever met. They told their dad anytime they saw someone skip class. And their dad was friends with my dad because

15

they went to high school together. So I just knew we were fucked.

"I can't even begin to tell you what all went down at that party. There was so much booze, weed, cocaine, and who knows what other kinds of drugs. All I know is I ended up in my parents' bed with two girls, one of them was the principal's daughter. All three of us are naked and doing our thing, when all of the sudden I hear police sirens. I knew there was nothing I could do. There was no way I was going to be able to get five hundred kids out of my house before the police got there. Plus my hands were a little full at the time, if you know what I mean. So I just decided to accept my fate and keep doing what I was doing.

"A few minutes later, a police officer knocked on the door of the room. I thought about ignoring it, but I knew that would only make things worse. I opened the door and saw that it was a female police officer. I don't remember exactly what I said or did, but the next thing I know, she joins us in the bed! That was probably the greatest accomplishment of my entire life.

"I don't know what the hell happened after that, but the next morning I woke up in a ditch wearing that officer's badge, cradling a dead dog, next to a leg-lamp. I dragged myself home and spent the next three days trying to clean up before my parents got back. I thought I had everything in pretty decent shape, but I still had all the neighbors to contend with. They had to have seen the police come to the door. I was ready to plead with them, beg, bribe them, whatever I had to do to get them to keep quiet about the party. But I found out that the neighbors actually showed up to the party and had such a good time that they decided that they weren't going to tell my parents about it. Best. Party. Ever."

Carlos sat dumbstruck, listening to every word Jordan slurred. Finally, after an uncomfortably long silence, Carlos said the only word he could muster: "Wow." How insightful.

Both men acted as if it was the greatest story in the history of the world. It was pathetic. If they heard just one of my stories, they would have worshipped the ground I walked on and offered to suck my dick to teach them my ways. Besides, my stories weren't half fabricated like the shit that came out of that hobbit's mouth.

"I know. It's one hell of a story. I can't believe I haven't told you it before," Jordan said.

"Me neither. Sounds like a great party!..." (incoherent Spanglish slurring) "...Mr. Tevan won't let you throw a work party."

Suddenly Jordan's fun-loving, carefree mood turned sullen. "I thought we weren't going to talk about work tonight."

"We're not, we're not. Sorry. I never should have brought that up."

"It's okay," Jordan said. His short legs impeded his ability to climb back onto his barstool. Once he was able to hoist himself up, Jordan quickly downed half of his beer before he spoke again. "It's just that he makes me so mad. I know I'm not always the most professional person, but I always get my work done. So what if I like to have a little fun while I'm doing it. Has that ever killed anyone?"

"I'm with you, man," Carlos replied. "He bugs me, too. He's always getting under my skin."

"What do you mean?" Jordan asked.

"It's the same thing you're saying. Seems like he's gotta big ole stick shoved up his ass. It's not our fault his ugly ass wife doesn't want to fuck him. He doesn't need to take his problems out on us. And he's always talking shit about me being Mexican and how I live in a one room apartment with twenty other people in my family."

"But you do live in a one room apartment with a bunch of your family members. And I say all that shit, too. Is that not okay?" Jordan feigned an apology. I could tell he didn't give a shit about his coworker's feelings, but most men were too big of pussies to show that to another man's face.

"No, you're fine with me, man. I like you. That asshole needs to learn to watch what he says. I don't know how much longer I can take his shit. Couple more comments and he'll be lucky if he only goes home with a busted nose."

"You know," Jordan started, "the best week I ever had at work was when Tevan had that heart attack."

"I'm with you on that. I just wish the old man would have kicked the bucket. I hate that pendejo."

"Me too, man, me too. I wish there was something I could do, but I can't quit. The pay is too good and I have a lot of bills."

"Same here. Not a lot of jobs for an illegal immigrant with no skills."

"Looks like we're stuck working for the bastard."

"Guess so."

"Unless someone took care of him."

As soon as they heard, both Jordan and Carlos looked around in bewilderment, neither of them having issued the statement.

"It was me, dumbasses," I proclaimed. Normally, I wouldn't have wasted my time talking to either of those two jackwagons, but they were so ripe for the picking that I couldn't resist. It was obvious their money wouldn't mean anything to me, but I needed to pay my tab at the country club, and they might at least make a dent in it. Besides, there weren't exactly people lining up for my services that night. And they'd be a hell of a lot easier than most. I can't normally threaten my clients with deportation. "Why don't you join me for a drink?"

Neither man dared refuse the offer. I knew they wouldn't. The panic in their eyes told me they were fearful that their boss would hear about their disparaging comments, as if I might somehow know the man. I had to fight back laughter at the notion. The thought of me associating with whomever their boss might be was beyond comical.

"You two must really hate your boss." Jordan and Carlos both shook their heads. How fucking stupid did they think I was? "There's no point pretending otherwise. I heard everything you said."

"You did?" Carlos asked, timidly.

"Yup. That was some pretty harsh stuff. Not the kind of things any boss would want to hear."

"Are you going to tell him?" Jordan asked. He tried to sound indifferent about the answer, but the tremble in his voice was music to my ears.

I chuckled. "Of course I'm not going to tell him. I don't even know who he is. And even if I did, I wouldn't say anything to him."

"Wait, you don't know him?" Carlos asked.

"No, I don't, ese."

"Then why did you want us to have a drink with you?" Jordan asked.

"Because, gentlemen, I think I may have a solution to your problem."

"A solution? What kind of solution?" Jordan asked.

I looked around to make sure that no one was within earshot. I didn't want to be overheard. "I know a guy that could make sure you never have to work for that man again."

"Now you're just being crazy. How could you do that?" Carlos asked.

"He'll get rid of the problem for you. You two both get to keep your jobs, but you don't have to work for that asshole anymore."

"What do you mean?" Jordan asked, his infinitesimal brain too underdeveloped to comprehend my implication. "How do we get to keep our jobs without working for him?"

"Do I have to spell it out for you two fucking imbeciles? Apparently I do." I hushed my voice to make certain that no one but Jordan and Carlos could hear me. "He'll kill your boss for you."

"Neither of us said we want him dead," Carlos said.

"You want to keep working for him, then? That's fine. I just thought I might be able to help. I'm going to get my tab and I'll be on my way."

Before I walked away from the table, Jordan stopped me. "I wouldn't mind if he was dead."

I sat back down, grinning, but I did not let Jordan or Carlos see. "Warming up to the idea?"

"Can the two of us talk alone for a second?" Jordan asked.

21

I took the opportunity to get another beer, and by the time I returned, a decision was made. "So, what did you two boys decide?"

Jordan looked at Carlos to confirm that he wanted to proceed as planned, and seeing the nod, he spoke. "We'd like to know a few more details about this."

"Of course. If you decide that you are interested, I will put you in touch with this person. He will contact you and tell you exactly what you need to do and what to bring. He'll take care of the rest from there. There will be no way to trace any of it back to either of you."

Jordan opened his mouth to respond, but Carlos beat him to it. "How much is this gonna cost us?"

"Ah, the elephant in the room," I began. "I cannot say I know exact numbers, but I do know that he is a reasonable man. Obviously, the target has to be taken into account. The more well-known or well-protected he is, the more it is going to cost. But the man also takes his clients into account. What I can tell you with you certainty is that he is a very fair man."

"What if we can't afford it or change our minds between now and then?" Jordan asked.

"If you change your minds, then the two of you go on your way, never to speak of it again. As for the price, I can assure you that you will be able to pay whatever price he asks of you."

Once more, Jordan looked at Carlos to make sure that they were on the same page, but he knew the answer, even before he saw the nod. "Let's do it."

"Just give me a way to have him contact you, and then we'll pretend this conversation never happened."

Jordan wrote down a phone number and handed it to me, after which I immediately left.

When I arrived back at my apartment, I stripped the wig and mustache off. Despite the fact that I'd consumed more than my fair share of beer at the bar, the Tylenol bottle in the bathroom cabinet remained untouched. Hangovers are for lesser men who can't handle their liquor.

I couldn't help but chuckle to myself as I sat on the edge of my bed. Those two idiots ate up every word I spoke. Sometimes I wondered how people were gullible enough to believe the steaming piles of bullshit I fed them. They had no idea they were throwing away their money, that I had absolutely no intention of killing their boss. Because I'm not actually a hitman.

Chapter 4

A few days later, I woke up with a smile on my face. It was Thursday, my favorite day of the week. It may sound unusual for Thursday to be anyone's favorite day of the week, but then again, I wasn't just anyone. I didn't work a *traditional* job like most people. For me, Thursday meant my weekly round of golf at the country club, followed by a trip to the racetrack for some exclusive betting on horseraces, and lastly I would enjoy a workout and steam at my gym.

Aside from being positioned exceptionally close to several bars, my apartment was also perfectly located for my Thursday activities. I lived close enough to the country club that I chose to walk each week. After that, I would catch a ride to the racetrack with Jim Bremer, one of the guys in my weekly foursome. From the racetrack, I could take a high-end commute service to the gym (offered to only the most prestigious members), which would also take me home, provided I didn't stop off at the bar. I didn't really like driving, especially because of all the traffic in the city. Finding parking was always a nightmare, and most days it was faster to walk, anyway. And my choice to walk and use the commute service allowed me to drink more. Between golfing and gambling, it was not unusual for me to finish a case of beer myself. After all that, I certainly needed to work out, especially if I wanted to keep up my physique for the ladies.

I walked out the front door of my apartment, then crossed the street. I turned right and came to an intersection where I waited for a gap in traffic to cross the street. Waiting for the 'walk' sign took too long. I strutted across the street, knowing that a driver would never dream of hitting me. As I did so, I saw something unusual ahead of me: a man standing on the corner. Not that it was unusual to pass people on the way to the country club, but, in all my time playing my weekly round of golf, I'd never seen a person at that particular intersection. Every shop in the immediate vicinity of the corner was out of business and it was not in an area with a lot of foot traffic.

The man was large, several inches taller than me, and he looked to be in exceptional physical condition. He was black with an unkempt, thick beard and messy black hair, not that

I need to specify the hair color (seriously, find me one exception). He wore disheveled clothes and held a sign written in such illegible chicken scratch that I couldn't make out what it said. He looked to be homeless, an assumption I was able to confirm when I crossed the street and got close enough to decipher the sign.

"Spare some change?" the man asked as I approached.

"Change? What's some change gonna get you? A gumball?" I replied.

"Do you have a dollar then? I'm sure *you* can scrape together one measly dollar."

"It's 2016. No one carries cash anymore."

I certainly could not blame the man for asking for money. I was, after all, very well-dressed. If anyone had the means to spare a dollar to the less fortunate, it was me. And I was not being entirely honest with the man, either. My wallet was almost overflowing with cash. But that was my gambling money. I didn't want to give it to some bum on the street. I had no interest in enabling the man. Surely, my donation would be squandered one way or another.

I walked into the clubhouse, not having encountered another person on the walk. The golf course did not spare any expense to make the clubhouse a popular hangout for its players. The interior strongly resembled a five star restaurant, with handcrafted chandeliers and tables made of the finest wood. The bar had a granite countertop and served nothing but top-shelf liquor. The walls were adorned with priceless relics from some of the game's greatest players.

I met my usual foursome (Jim Bremer, Phil Kinney, and Roland Weatherly) for our traditional pre-round drink(s). As I liked to say, "golf can only be frustrating if you're sober enough to let it get to your head".

As I shared a drink with the three men, I looked around the clubhouse. There were several people I recognized but did not know personally. A fat, bald man sat with a skinny elderly man, loudly recalling a story from his weekend of debauchery reserved only for the hardened, affluent sadists they feature in horror movies. A few tables away sat another group consisting of a muscular man in his mid-thirties; a young, lanky man; a man with a bald head and gray beard who looked he could have been the lanky man's father; and a man around the same age with a thick mustache. The man with the mustache looked familiar. I knew I recognized him from somewhere other than the country club, but I couldn't quite place him.

After the drink (and three rounds of shots at my urging), we went outside. The exterior of the clubhouse and the course itself were, if anything, even more extravagant than the interior of the clubhouse. The entranceway to the course blocked a large bronze gate. Just past it, a stone cobbled road led to the clubhouse, the driving range, and the first tee box. The course was meticulously cared for; not a single blade of grass was out of place. A large stone wall surrounded the course, blocking any view from the public. As a matter of fact, only the course employees, members, and those lucky enough to be invited to play a round with one of the members had ever seen the course. It was even more exclusive than Augusta National, and I wouldn't have had it any other way.

Once the round was over, I got in Jim's car, a fully customized Tesla Model S, to make our way to the racetrack. On this particular day, I was more upset than usual after a round of golf. I shot a disappointing three-over par and lost three hundred dollars in various bets throughout the round, much of which was in the wallet of the man driving the car I rode in. Jim's continued razzing did nothing to improve my mood.

When we got to the racetrack, my anger had subsided. I had a knack for picking winning horses, so I was confident that I was going to win back my money, plus more. There were only a few dozen other men present at the track. One of them was the man with the mustache from the golf course. He'd been at the track on a few other occasions, so his appearance did not come as a total surprise. As I noticed the man, however, I could have sworn he looked at me, but he looked away before I could be certain.

I placed my bet, then took a seat next to Jim in the stands. My horse was in the fourth lane. I stared at it as we waited for the race to begin. A few seconds later, the starter pistol fired and the stables burst open. I was bubbling with excitement, but that soon burst. My horse stumbled coming out of the gate. Before it regained its balance, it was more than ten lengths behind the lead horse and well behind the others. I shook my head in disgust. The horse did not give up as easily, though. It raced to catch up to the others, and, halfway around the track, the gap lessened considerably. The horse was clearly the fastest of the lot, moving so quickly it was like it was gliding across the track. Suddenly, it caught up to one horse. Then another. As it rounded the third corner, the horse moved into fifth place. Only the straightaway remained. I sat on the edge of my seat as I watched. I couldn't believe that my horse stood a chance. The jockey urged the horse to go faster, propelling it into fourth place, but that was all the better it would finish. There just wasn't enough distance left for my horse to finish in the money.

After the race ended, I turned to Jim and said, "It's just my luck that I pick the fastest horse, but he's too stupid to make it out of the gates. I didn't know horses could be fucking retarded."

"I really thought he was going to catch up," Jim replied, sincerely for once.

"Me too. If I wanted to be teased like that I would head down to Sugar Daddy's and dry hump some strippers. I'd probably lose the same amount of money, but at least that way I'd get to see some tits."

Never one to dwell on the past or worry about lost money, I left the stands to place a bet on the next race. The betting counter was only a few steps away from the bottom of the stands, but there were a few people in line, so I had to wait before I could place my wager. Normally, I'm not one to wait in lines, but this was one of the few places where I did not receive preferential treatment. I was amongst equals. Or at least the only people that could be mentioned as my equals.

As I waited in line, something caught my eye. Five people stood between me and the counter, but I could have sworn the man from the country club stared at me as he cashed out. The man was gone, though, when I turned back to him. He gave me an eerie feeling, but I didn't dwell on it long, as I was called to the counter a few moments later.

The rest of the races did not go much better. I won money on two races, but lost on four others, losing just under $1,000 in total. All in all, it was far from the worst day I ever had golfing and gambling. But I hate to lose. I didn't care so much about the money – it was negligible as far as I was concerned – but nothing gets me in a worse mood than losing. My ultra-competitiveness often came back to bite me in the ass.

Every fifteen minutes, the high-end commute service ran between the golf course, the racetrack, the gym, and several other places in town. I entered the first car that pulled up (door already opened for me) and relaxed on my way to the gym.

There were two reasons that I liked going to the gym, and neither of them was because I wanted to stay healthy. One of the reasons that I liked going to the gym was because of the girls. Girls always appreciated a man with a chiseled body, and I was more than willing to provide them with that. The other reason was that it allowed me to blow off some steam after a day of losses (which had been happening far too frequently).

The gym was not crowded – it never was on Thursdays, nor any other day for that matter. That was one of the perks of belonging to one of the most exclusive gyms in the area. There were no 'New Year's Resolutioners' crowding the gym for two weeks, only to quit when they realize that their goal was unattainable. No morbidly obese people who couldn't run more than a mile without having a heart attack, leaving sweat marks on everything they touched. No wannabes lifting for five minutes and spending the next hour walking around the gym and looking at themselves in the mirror. No, this was not your typical discount franchise gym with worn machinery and crusty shower curtains. Though, at this point, I hardly feel like I need to explain that to you. Could you really imagine *me* in a gym, shoulder-to-shoulder with other people running on treadmills, racing around in between lifts to make sure that I was able to get a bench?

I put in five miles on the treadmill, then proceeded to use the bench press, do some curls and the shoulder press, then several other machines to work my upper body (no, I didn't skip leg day, that was on Tuesdays). I finished my upper body lifts, then ended with an ab workout. It wasn't my favorite thing to do, but it sure kept the ladies happy. Any guy that tells you that he is lifting because he wants to get stronger or wants to get in better shape is more full of shit than a constipated elephant. Everything – and I mean *everything* – guys do is to impress girls. That's why they let themselves go *after* they get married.

The last thing I did before leaving the gym was go to the steam room. It was a relaxing way to finish my workout. Everyone at the gym knew that I liked my peace and quiet when I went to the steam room, so I was always able to have the whole room to myself. It allowed me the opportunity to be alone with my thoughts for a few minutes and saved me from seeing other guys' sweaty balls.

Halfway through my time in the steam room, the door opened. Generally, once an intruder saw who was in there, he would contritely leave, wishing he'd never opened the door. Surprisingly, though, the man did not leave. Instead, he spoke to me. The steam had fogged the room so much that it was impossible to make out who the person was, but his voice sounded vaguely familiar.

"Mr. Donahue, I have some business to discuss with you."

Chapter 5

I squinted hard, trying to make out his face. The audacity of this bastard was unbelievable. Not only did he interrupt my steam, but he knew my real name and wanted to discuss business with me. Clearly this man didn't know who he was dealing with. Though he must have known something about me if he knew my name. I only had one thing to say back to him.

"Who the fuck are you?"

Apparently those were the magic words because the man moved close enough for me to see him, revealing that he was the older man from the golf course and the racetrack. He was still wearing a suit. He didn't come to the gym to workout. He followed me, and that agitated me more than the fact that he interrupted my steam. "My name is Gordon Stanton. A client of mine is interested in your services," he said.

There were so many rumors about what I did for a living that I honestly had no idea which Gordon Stanton chose to believe. However, in my experience, men who looked like him often sought to purchase services that could make even the most seasoned prostitute blush...or cringe. What I did know was that he was going to go home disappointed because no one knew what services I could actually provide. "Services? I'm afraid I don't know what you're talking about."

"I am not a fool, Mr. Donahue, so please do not treat me like one. We both know what you do for a living." As he spoke, I could not help but notice the ring on his right pinky finger. It looked to be made of solid gold with a magnificent red diamond.

"There are many rumors about me."

"Rumors are just that. I have never put any stock in them. I know what you do and I would bet that I am one of few people. For good reason." He must have seen the look on my face and realized that I was not going to give up any information willingly because he continued. "You are a man that can get things done, a man that can make problems go away. My client is willing to pay handsomely to make their problem go away. If you do not wish to help, that is fine, but please stop treating me like a fool."

My face was stoic as he spoke, but secretly my insides were doing front flips. How on earth could he know what I did? I had always been so careful to conceal my identity, so careful to make sure that nothing could be traced back to me. There was nothing, no way. Yet, somehow he knew. But how?

I knew that he would never tell me, so I continued the conversation. "Let's say I am interested in helping you, how much money are we talking?"

"$500,000," he said. "I have half of it with me now. You will get the other half when the task is complete."

Fortunately, hiding my emotions was one of my strong points because if not, I wouldn't have been able to stop grinning. $500,000?! That was more than I had ever received for any one assignment. Actually, it was more like $250,000 because there was no way I was going to earn the second half of the money, but it was still far more than I'd ever been paid. Still, I knew that I had to play it cool, otherwise he may think something was up. "I think we might be able to work something out," I said, extending my hand for him to shake, but a thought popped into my mind as I did so. "Who is your associate?"

"I was hoping that you would not ask that question, Mr. Donahue. My client requested absolute anonymity. If that is a problem for you, then I am sure that we will be able to find another person with comparable skills."

How stupid was I? Of course someone willing to pay that sum of money would want to remain anonymous. Hopefully I didn't ruin my chances. "A problem? No, not at all. I completely understand the desire to remain anonymous." This was not a lie at all. I truly did understand because I wanted to make sure that I remained anonymous as well. *Clearly* that was working for me.

"That is excellent news. I am going to excuse myself now. When you get to your locker you'll find a briefcase with $250,000, as well as a phone loaded with as much information as we could gather on the subject and a phone number you can reach me at. You made the right decision, Mr. Donahue."

Gordon Stanton walked out of the steam room, leaving me alone. As much as I liked spending my steams alone, I wouldn't complain if each one had the same result as that. $250,000? I could not believe it. I was actually going to be paid $250,000...to do absolutely nothing. Of course, he didn't need to know that.

I finished my steam more relaxed than any other steam I'd ever had. It is an indescribable feeling to know that $250,000 is waiting for you in your gym locker. As soon as I was done, I walked out of the steam room with extra gusto to claim my newfound riches. And who could blame me?

When I got to my locker I soon found out that Gordon Stanton was not lying. Two items waited for me, neither of which I placed there: a brown, leather briefcase and a cell phone. I opened the briefcase and saw that it was full of money. I pocketed the cell phone and walked out the front door, briefcase in hand.

Chapter 6

In the grand scheme of things, $250,000 wasn't a large sum of money to me, but it wasn't every day that I was handed a quarter of a million dollars. That meant some of the money had to be spent. And I knew just how to do it.

I looked down at my watch as I left the gym. It was only three-fifty-five in the afternoon. Some people might consider that too early to start drinking, but I'd started early in the morning. Why stop now?

I walked into my favorite bar, The Scorpion, where everyone knew me as John Glasson, and sat in my usual spot.

"What'll it be today?" the bartender, Ricky, asked.

"I'll have a double whiskey sour, Ricky. And get everyone another round on me while you're at it."

I set two crisp one hundred dollar bills on the bar from my newfound riches and waited for my drink. Less than a minute later, Ricky returned, a whiskey sour in hand. "Is this for the drinks?" he asked, picking up the two bills.

"No, Ricky, I just saw how well you poured my drink and I thought that you did such a nice a job that you earned a two hundred dollar tip."

"Really?" he asked. Needless to say, Ricky wasn't exactly the smartest guy out there. Hence why he had a job as a bartender.

It took everything in me to resist making another sarcastic comment. "No, Ricky, that's for the drinks for the rest of the bar."

"Oh, I just didn't know because that's way more than it's going to cost for those drinks. There's only five other people in here."

I had to give Ricky the benefit of the doubt on that one. Two hundred dollars was a lot to spend on drinks for six people, but Ricky did not know about my recent fortunes. Still, I was not going to give him the satisfaction of realizing that he was right to think that my payment was a little out of the ordinary. That goes against everything I believe in.

"Oh, my mistake. I can take one of those bills back if you'd prefer a smaller tip." I knew that would put him in his place. Both Ricky and I knew that I wouldn't take back any of the money, but it was still fun to mess with him and make him worry that I might.

"No, no, that's not what I meant at all. I was just trying to let you know that it's been unusually slow today."

"Unusually slow? For a Thursday? Hmm, seems just about the same as any other Thursday."

"I meant tip-wise," he said.

"Now you're starting to catch on, Ricky. That's the kind of quick-witted response I expect to see out of you."

I always got a kick out of messing with Ricky. He was the bartender at The Scorpion on Thursdays, and more often than not, I ended up there after my workout. Drinking back all the calories you burned working out is the definition of a balanced lifestyle.

Ricky set my drink in front of me and I downed it one gulp. "Keep 'em coming, Ricky. It's gonna be a good night."

As the night went on, the bar started to fill up. The Scorpion was never one of the busiest bars in the area - that was one of the reasons that I liked to go there - but the atmosphere was always good, and, as the bar filled, ladies came.

By seven, it was no longer just me and four other guys. I could think of no better way to celebrate than bringing a girl home. I searched around the bar for an hour, trying to pick the right girl. I wasn't just looking for the hottest girl in the bar. No, I was much more calculated than that. I had to make sure that I found a girl that would be gullible enough to believe in the John Gasson persona and who wouldn't get too attached. There was nothing worse than a one night stand that thought sex meant you were in a committed relationship.

Lady Luck must have finished PMSing because she was finally starting to swing to my side. Just after I'd decided to move on to another bar, the perfect target sat down beside me. She was gorgeous. When she smiled the whole room seemed to get brighter. Her long, blonde hair perfectly complimented her sexy legs. And that dress. It was just long enough to cover everything, but short enough that it didn't leave too much to the imagination. And that's not even mentioning her ass and tits (you didn't really think I was a gentleman, did you?). They were perfectly shaped and it took everything in me not to stare. Her ass was so big that half of it hung off the bar stool. And her tits stuck out so far that she wouldn't have needed a plate at all. She could have just set her food right on them. Everything about her fit my criteria. Her blonde hair meant that she was going to believe every word I told her (yes, the dumb blonde stereotype is true, trust me). And no one dressed like that unless they were looking for some action. She was like a dragon waiting to be slayed and I was King Arthur, carrying Excalibur with me in my pants.

"Can I buy you a drink?" I asked, focusing all my effort on making eye contact with her.

"Of course," she seductively replied. Just like that, I knew I was in. Still, I knew that she was going to make me go through the motions. They always did.

"What's your name?" I asked. I didn't care what her name was, and I didn't even listen long enough to hear her answer. I think it started with an M. Marie, maybe.

"And your last name?" If it was possible, I cared about this even less, but girls always got a kick out of it when I pretended to know someone with the same last name as them.

"Do you really think we need last names?" I almost came on the spot. This girl was everything I could have hoped for.

"I like the way you think, M..." I pulled a George Costanza and muffled the rest of her name. "My name is John." I'm not even sure she heard me say that. I could have said I was Tyrion of house Lannister for all she cared.

We finished our drinks and ordered another round. We talked, but neither of us cared what the other's answers were. They weren't important. We were just waiting until the moment felt right for us to slip out of the bar together. After the third drink, Maggie (or was it Megan?) or whatever her name was excused herself to go to the bathroom. I knew that was the signal. I gave Ricky two more one hundred dollar bills, and waited for my entertainment for the night to return. As I waited, I decided to look through the phone that Gordon Stanton left me.

Normally, I didn't like to work at the bar, but I had nothing better to do and I was willing to do anything to avoid another conversation with Ricky. I was surprised by how much information Gordon Stanton included. There were thorough entries about the man's past and education. It was just too bad all of that work was for naught. I scrolled through the pages, skimming for any interesting pieces of information. I stopped when I came across a picture of the man. I stared at it for what seemed like ten minutes. That face. It seemed so familiar. Then suddenly it came to me. I saw that man for the first time earlier that day. Awestruck, I walked out of the bar, completely forgetting about Morgan (Mandy?) in the bathroom.

Chapter 7

I was too drunk to think any more about the man that night - way too drunk. But the next morning, I pulled out the phone again to be sure of what I saw. I looked at the picture for more than fifteen minutes before deciding that my mind wasn't playing tricks on me. I was looking at a picture of the homeless man I met on the way to the golf course.

I usually didn't take a strong interest in my 'targets', but something about that man stuck out to me. He intrigued me. More than that, a sudden wave of curiosity overtook me. Why on earth would someone be willing to pay $500,000 to have a homeless man killed? Surely someone would have been able to do it for significantly less than what I was being paid.

As I continued to read the background information, I found out more about the man. His name was Robert Tindall and he was originally from Pittsburgh. And...wait...he was college educated? At the University of Florida?! I mean, it wasn't Harvard, but how many homeless people could tout a college degree? It was bizarre.

I read on, thinking that Gordon Stanton and his associate may have made a mistake, but the story only became stranger. Robert Tindall was employed by a large financial services company. He'd been nominated for a bunch of different awards that I'd never heard of. Everything about him seemed normal, making this whole situation all the more confusing. And the worst part was, there was no more information about him, nothing to explain how a businessman that seemed to have a stable career was now homeless. Nothing to explain why he was now designated for murder.

I'd never been so intrigued by one of the people I was hired to kill. Usually, it was a scorned lover like Colonel Sanders or someone that was mad at their boss like the kids from the bar earlier that week. Occasionally, there would be someone that had a different reason, but I never paid them much attention. I wasn't going to be killing them anyway, so what did I care who the people were or why someone wanted them dead? This was not the case with Robert Tindall. I was interested in him. He sparked a curiosity in me. Something about him didn't seem to add up, and I had to find out why.

I scrolled through the phone several more times, hoping to catch something that I might have overlooked. Finally, after my fifth or sixth time through it, I opened the contacts. Only one contact was listed: *Help.* I clicked on it.

"Hello," the voice on the other end of the line said. I didn't need two guesses to know that it was Gordon Stanton. "Do you have a plan in place?"

"I'm working on it," I lied.

"What can I help you with, Mr. Donahue?"

"What did this guy do to earn a death wish?"

"You don't get paid to ask questions. You get paid to do a job. Don't call again unless you have a real problem." He hung up before I had a chance to say anything else.

Maybe Gordon Stanton wouldn't answer any questions over the phone, but he might be more willing to talk if I paid him a visit. A quick internet search showed that there were four Gordon Stanton's in town. I didn't have the time nor the patience to go to all four of their addresses. That meant it was time to pay a visit to my old friend, Trevor.

He didn't live within walking distance of my place, so, against my will, I was forced to drive. I went to the underground garage beneath my apartment complex and hopped in my 2016 Camaro. As much as I disliked driving, it was tough to match the thrill of taking that beauty down south to a small town highway to see how fast I could get it going. My record was 158, but I was pretty sure I could beat that if I was able to find a road that had a long enough straightaway.

I drove across town until I came to Trevor's apartment complex. He lived in one of the worst parts of town. It was overrun with gangbangers, hookers, and drug dealers. I never liked to leave my car there very long. Who knows what those low life pieces of shit would do to it. Steal it? Take the rims or the tires? Tag it with graffiti in their never-ending turf war? I wasn't sure which was worse, so I always made sure my visits were short.

I knocked on the door and waited for a response. I heard footsteps and what sounded like someone looking through the eyehole. "What the fuck do you want?" he asked. Maybe calling him a friend wasn't exactly accurate.

"Let me in."

"Why the fuck would I do that?"

"Because I have $1,000 for you if you do." The door flew open as soon as heard me say "dollars".

Trevor Fillmore was tall and lanky, and his hair was always a mess. His apartment was even worse. There were months-old dirty dishes scattered everywhere, trash and fast food bags thrown all over the floor, and other random shit on the couch and on the floor that took up so much room that you had to kick half of it out of the way to be able to walk anywhere.

In the back of the living room, just barely visible from the front door, was the reason I was there. It was also the only thing in the apartment that was ever kept clean. A massive computer sat below a table that was covered with three monitors. Trevor and I may not have always seen eye-to-eye on things, but he possessed skills I did not have. He called himself a hacker, but Trevor provided infinitely more value than that. I'd never seen someone command such a mastery of cybersecurity and computer coding. He could gain access to any supposedly secure database, website, or file with ease. Anytime I had trouble finding dirt on someone, I made a trip to Trevor's, and he always found a silver bullet for me. I couldn't even begin to fathom how much money and time I'd been able to save because of Trevor's information. That's one of the risks of being a hit man that doesn't actually kill anyone. Sometimes you have to dig for dirt to blackmail someone, and no one was better at that than Trevor.

Trevor took a seat behind his computer desk, already knowing the nature of my visit. He still had a hose wrapped around his left arm. The heroin clouded his mind, causing him to forget even the most simple things, like removing the evidence of his crippling drug addiction. I didn't mind that he was high, though. If anything, I preferred it. Trevor did his best work when he was high.

"Name," he said. Trevor wanted me to get me out of his apartment just as much as I wanted to leave.

"I don't need any dirt today, Trevor. I just need you to help me find someone. His name is Gordon Stanton."

Trevor started to work his magic. "It looks like there's four of them here in town and ten more in the surrounding area. Do you have any more information?"

"Do you have pictures of these guys? I'd be able to ID him from a picture."

It took a little longer this time, but Trevor had some pictures for me after a few minutes. I looked through all the pictures of the Gordon Stanton's from the city and then from the surrounding area, but none of them were a match for the one I met. "What else do you know about this guy?"

I thought for a minute, then it came to me. The country club. Of course! "He's a member of the country club with me," I said.

Trevor did some more digging, screwing up his face as he worked hard to unearth this piece of information. He knew that I would not pay him unless he was able to find some usable piece of information, and $1,000 would surely buy a lot of heroin. He shook his head and slammed his fist on the table. "There's no Gordon Stanton on any membership list and there are no cameras in the vicinity, so I can't even find some pictures for you."

At that moment, it finally occurred to me that Gordon Stanton had done exactly what I'd been doing for years. He gave me a fake name. I never saw it coming. He was definitely much smarter than I gave him credit for. Still, I knew one more thing about him. "What about this?" I asked, pulling out the phone Gordon Stanton gave me.

Trevor plugged the phone into his computer. If we were going to find out any piece of useful information, it would be on the phone.

It didn't take long for me to realize the phone was a lost cause. Trevor dejectedly unplugged the phone, and the look on his face confirmed my suspicions. "The phone won't even show up on my computer. It's encrypted beyond a level I've ever seen. The number's no good, either. It's a burner. Completely untraceable. It was paid in cash, so there's no trail."

It was my turn to slam my fists on the table. If Trevor couldn't find out who this guy was, what hope did I have?

"Look up one other thing for me. See if you can find any information about this guy." I flipped through the phone until I came to the picture of Robert Tindall.

I didn't want to leave Trevor's apartment completely empty-handed, and I still hadn't been able to get Robert

Tindall off my mind since I first saw his picture. There had to be some piece of information I was missing.

Trevor searched through the computer for the better part of fifteen minutes, but when he spoke, his sullen tone told me the answer.

"I couldn't find anything about him. Nothing at Florida, nothing from the company he worked for, nothing for any of the prizes. Jack shit."

I threw $500 on the table and walked to the door.

"I thought you said you were going to pay me $1,000."

"And I thought I was going to leave here knowing more than before I came."

Chapter 8

I got to my car and saw that it hadn't been touched. I drove away as quickly as I could, squealing my tires on the way out. I parked in the garage and started for my apartment, but stopped before I got to the elevator. I couldn't let the day be a complete waste. I walked out of the garage and down the street toward the country club. Maybe someone there could confirm the real identity of Gordon Stanton.

As I walked, I saw the homeless man standing on the same street corner as the previous day. I was two blocks away, but there was no mistaking him. That was Robert Tindall, if that actually was his name. I was beginning to doubt the validity of anything in the file.

I walked to the opposite side of the street, so that he wouldn't notice me. As I got closer, I was torn about what to do. Should I continue on my path to the golf course or should I watch Robert and see if I could find out any more information about him? As I closed in on him, I made my decision. I ducked into the hotel that stood kitty-corner from the homeless man.

"Can I get a room for a few hours?" I asked as I approached the desk.

The lady behind the desk looked to be in her mid-forties. She stuck up her nose in disgust at my request. "This isn't that kind of hotel," she scoffed.

For a brief moment, I found her comment humorous. But the more I thought about it, the more offended I became. Did I look like the type of man that needed to pay a hooker to have sex with him? Sure, a lot of wealthy men indulged in that, but those were the fat, rancid pigs. Being both handsome and wealthy made the payment unnecessary.

"I'm not meeting some cheap whore up there," I said, "unless you want to join me. And in that case," I looked through my wallet to see how much cash I had, "I only have two bucks left...actually, that seems more than fair."

Her death glare lit my soul on fire, but she chose not to respond. Finally I handed her my credit card. "Charge me for a full night if you have to. I don't give a shit. I just want a room that faces this direction." I pointed to the street where Robert Tindall stood.

She looked confused about the request, but kept her mouth shut as she finished the transaction. That was probably in her best interest. A few minutes later, I had a key and I was on my way up to my room.

Despite the front desk clerk's clear impatience for my attitude, I had to admit she found me the perfect room. Frankly, I couldn't care less about any of the amenities, but the view was absolutely perfect. The street corner that Robert Tindall stood on was well within my field of vision. Now the surveillance started.

This was far from my first foray into surveillance. It might look fun on TV, but let me tell you, it's a hell of a lot more boring than you'd expect. I watched Robert stand on the street corner begging for money from everyone who walked past him in disgust. He hardly moved, did nothing out of the ordinary, didn't throw any of his own feces. That only confused me further. There had to be some reason this man was homeless.

After spending almost an hour within a five foot radius, Robert was on the move. He scooped some money from the jack-o-lantern bucket that he used to collect his donations and walked into the grocery store that was just two blocks behind him. No surprise. There was a liquor store inside. He returned five short minutes later, not carrying a bottle of booze like I expected, but instead eating a sandwich and holding a bag of chips. That was odd. What kind of homeless man didn't take any and every opportunity to score himself some alcohol?

I continued to watch, but it was more of the same. Robert stood begging for anything that people could spare. Occasionally, someone would throw some money into the hat in front of him or stop to chat with him, and Robert smiled and appeared to thank them.

Several hours later, he made another trip to the grocery store. Surely this time he would return with a bottle of booze. Again, I was proven incorrect. He walked out carrying something else to eat, but this time I couldn't quite make out what it was.

As I watched Robert, he continued to intrigue me. He didn't drink alcohol and seemed surprisingly lucid. He was nothing like any other homeless man I'd ever seen. I was by no means an expert in homelessness, but I knew there had to be something more to Robert.

Just before nightfall, he was on the move again. This time, however, Robert walked in my direction. He crossed the street and then I lost sight of him. I tried moving closer to the window but it was no use. I lost him. I waited at the window for several minutes, thinking that he would reappear when he was finished doing whatever he was doing. Then I was met with a knock at the door.

Before I opened the door, I looked through the eyehole. I nearly shit my pants when I saw Robert Tindall's face on the other side of the door. I thought for a second about whether I should open the door or not, but sensed I was in no immediate danger.

"Why have you been watching me all day?" he asked when I finally opened the door.

Chapter 9

I hadn't paid much attention to Robert Tindall's appearance when I first encountered him, but I'd studied his picture in the file tirelessly. Aside from having a more aged look and a slightly more disheveled appearance, he looked identical to the man in the picture. His clothes were starting to get tattered from excessive wear, but they still looked as though he spent as much as time as he could making them look presentable (though a ripped college t-shirt and badly stained sweatpants are hardly what I would typically call "presentable").

I motioned for Robert to walk in the room and offered him a place to sit on the bed. "Why have you been watching me?" he asked again.

I thought about my answer for a moment, then cooly said, "I was hired to kill you."

"I'm starting to think that coming up here was a bad idea." He did not seem phased by my answer. Nor did he seem scared or worried. As a matter of fact, he seemed utterly nonchalant.

"I'm not going to do it, though," I said, to make sure that he did not take off on me.

"I know."

"You do?" I was not thrilled about the prospect of yet another person knowing my secret

"If you were going to kill me, you would have done it already." A sense of relief passed over me.

Robert waited for my answer, but I didn't oblige him. He seemed sharp, witty, exactly like I would have expected a prominent businessman to be. So why the hell was he homeless?

Once he saw that I was not going to reply to his statement, he spoke again. "So who sent you to kill me?"

"I was going to ask you the same thing."

"You don't know who hired you?"

I recanted the story of my encounter with Gordon Stanton, how I tried to discover his identity, how I had no idea who he was working for, and how everything about it bewildered me.

"So you don't know anyone that might want you dead?" I asked when I finished telling the tale.

"Yes and no." The guy was a fucking enigma. Nothing about him made sense.

I tried not to let my confusion show when I asked, "What?"

"It's kind of a long story," he said.

"Well I'm free for the night and you clearly have nowhere to be, so get to talking."

"The thing is, I'm not exactly sure myself. There are parts of it that I still don't understand, but I'll tell you everything I know." He paused and took a deep breath. I could tell from his tone and hesitation that he had told few people this story, maybe nobody. But he started. "I don't know how much you know about me, so I'll just start from the beginning.

"I graduated from the University of Florida in the late nineties with a degree in business management. I was heavily recruited, with offers from just about every major financial services company and several of the largest banks in the country. Though the banking jobs intrigued me, I'd always been drawn to investing, so I took a job as a financial advisor.

"I was damn good at it, too. After just three years, I boasted a portfolio worth more than fifty million dollars, my investments consistently earning some of the top returns in the entire company. But just when I was hitting my peak, it all came crashing down.

"I made a series of bad investments and lost almost half the value of my portfolio. Nearly every one of my clients withdrew their money and either switched to another advisor within my company or to one of my competitors. After that, my company had no choice but to fire me. I'd lost them millions of dollars and cost them some of their most loyal clients.

"I tried to get another job in financial services, but no one wanted to hire someone with such a glaring black mark on their record. That came as no surprise. Truthfully, I wouldn't have hired me either.

"When I realized that I no longer had a future in my dream job, I tried to go to my fallback of banking, but even they wouldn't hire me. I started to apply for various management jobs, especially those did not deal with investment or money management. With my experience and resume, I should have been more than qualified for any of those positions, but each and every one of them came up with an excuse not to hire me. And that's where things really start to get weird.

"Once I'd accepted the fact that my career in business was effectively over, I tried to get a job in construction, maintenance, and essentially anything else that could pay the bills. But still, I remained unemployed. I even tried to get a job at McDonald's flipping burgers, but even they wouldn't hire me. It honestly felt like someone had not only blackballed me in the finance industry, but was also doing anything and everything they could to ensure that I'd never get hired again.

"That was the lowest point of my life. I spiraled into a deep, dark depression. It got so bad that I tried to kill myself, but things were going so poorly for me that I couldn't even fucking do that right.

"I'd built myself a pretty decent nest egg, but it didn't take me long to burn through that. Less than a year after I was fired, I lost my house. I've been homeless ever since. I still apply for jobs and keep holding out hope that someone will give me another chance, but no one has. At least not yet."

I waited to see if Robert had anything else to add, but he didn't. It was a good thing I was sitting for the tale because it was one of the most bizarre stories I'd ever been told. My immediate reaction was to dismiss it. The man sounded like a compulsive liar. Maybe he was afflicted with some undiagnosed mental disorder. That would explain a lot. Or maybe it was none of those. As certifiable as Robert sounded, I sensed something else, something that seemed an awful lot like genuinity. As fucking ludicrous as the story sounded, I couldn't shake that feeling. He did corroborate a lot of what was included in file. Though, in fairness, I'd been skeptical of that from the start. But something about Robert made me want to believe him. How was it that I - the master of deception, the chronic teller of outlandish stories - could be convinced that even one word Robert said might be true?

Might. That was the keyword. It only might be true. In some way having that sense of doubt scared me. I prided myself on decisiveness and my ability to wade through heaping piles of bullshit. Yet, somehow, I was unable to certainly convince myself whether this man's story was true. What I did know was that his story at least made me curious to find out more, and more than ever I wanted to find out who hired me to kill him.

Chapter 10

By the time Robert finished telling the story it was nearly ten o'clock. I was ready to get back home, but now I had another problem: what the hell was I going to do about Robert? I needed to keep him close, make sure he didn't try to make a run for it. After all, someone wanted him dead. But I wasn't in the business of doing favors for others. I weighed the pros and cons, ultimately deciding it was in my best interest to get Robert a room. He could still slip away unbeknownst to me, but this was the only way there'd be even a sliver of a chance that I'd see him again.

"I'm going to head back to my apartment. I think we should meet up again tomorrow morning," I said.

"I'd like that. I should probably get back too."

"Not so fast. I'm not going to let you sleep on the ground tonight."

"No, no, that's far too kind of you. This place is too nice. I couldn't possibly ask that from you."

"Good, because I wouldn't let you stay here, not when they have my credit card. I'm already worried that they're going to bill me for your homelessness leaving a mark on the room. Here, take this." I reached into my wallet and handed the man a hundred dollar bill. "There ought to be a motel that is more suited to your style somewhere around here. That should be more than enough for the night. Meet me out on that corner at nine o'clock tomorrow morning."

"Gee...thanks...that sure is kind of you."

He did not even bother to mask the sarcasm in his voice. I thought I was being nice, giving him a place to sleep, but it wasn't worth my time to argue about that. I left the room without saying another word, and the sound of the door closing let me know that Robert was not far behind me.

Before Robert and I parted ways, I told him that I wanted to go to the country club to try to find Gordon Stanton. For some reason, he was adamant about coming with, so, after much protest, I begrudgingly allowed him to join. I assured him that the country club was a very upscale place that had very strict etiquette and handed him another one hundred dollar bill, which was my way of telling him to get some new fucking clothing so that he could at least look as though he belonged in the same zip code as the clubhouse. Apparently that wasn't direct enough.

My reaction to seeing Robert return the next morning was a mixture of anger, confusion, and pity, with a strong urge to laugh. It was a very strange feeling, one that I don't think I'd ever felt or ever will feel again. He stood proudly on the same street corner where I'd first seen him, wearing what only he could call his best suit. He wore a plain white t-shirt. On top of that, he wore a mint green blazer with small holes every few inches. And somehow the pants were worse. They were silver and sequenced, at least four inches too short. It looked like he went dumpster diving in the back of Paisley Park. Yet, there he proudly stood.

Only with willpower stronger than a pissed off ox on steroids could I resist commenting on the outfit. And who could blame me for sparing his feelings? Surely Robert didn't have much to be proud of. There was no need for me to say something that would take away a rare good feeling for him. "How's it going?" I asked, looking down the moment the words left my mouth, quickly feigning an attempt to tie my shoe, but really trying to compose my laughter.

"I'm great," he said, opening up his mouth into a toothy grin that surely was larger than he'd smiled in several years.

Try as I might, I just was not able to contain myself from letting a small chuckle escape at the sight of that. I have to admit though, I was proud that I didn't let more than that out. That was one of the funniest things I'd seen in years...the naivety in his grin was priceless.

"For all of five seconds. Then right back to shitty." He, apparently, did not share my opinion that it took great restraint to avoid laughter. He, for some reason, took offense to the chuckle.

"What's the matter? What are you so upset about?" I asked, as we began to walk.

"Upset? Me? Why would you think that?"

"Well, you stopped smiling, for one. And you haven't blinked in at least a minute for two. But the fact that you've been flipping me off for the last hundred yards was what really clued me in."

"Don't you know what..."

"Sarcasm is? *Noooooo*, I have *nooooo* idea what sarcasm is."

"If you have a problem with the way I'm dressed, you can just say something."

"I don't have a problem with the way you're dressed. But I would like to know what you did what the hundred dollars I gave you if you didn't spend it on a new suit."

"I don't accept charity."

"What about the money I gave you for a motel? Where did you sleep last night? And what about the other hundred dollars?" Robert looked through his journal, obviously ignoring my questions. "And what about that bucket you put on the street? Wouldn't you call that charity?"

Robert turned his head, pretending to be enthralled by the sign of a local diner so that he did not have to respond. It was not his ignoring my questioning that bothered me, but rather his complete hypocrisy and inconsistency.

"So you do take some charity?" I asked, challenging him to disagree with me.

As we walked (and begrudgingly talked), I quickly realized that Robert was not some poor homeless man that I should feel bad for. No, he was nothing even close to that. He'd compelled me with his story and must have held back showing any real personality, because our conversation made it abundantly clear that he was a real prick. He disagreed with every single thing that I said, no matter how trivial the matter. I think I could have suggested that his dick was eight inches soft and he would have come up with some argument about why small dicks were better.

The more we walked, the less I felt sorry for him and the more I felt sorry for me. He was such an asshole that I wanted to leave him behind at every street corner that we passed. But I knew I couldn't. He was still a flight risk and there was every chance he'd be too stupid to find his way back to the motel. So I led Robert, completely against my will, all the way to the gates of my country club.

As soon as we got to the gates (which were guarded by two large men on the ground and two large watchtowers on both sides), I tried to casually leave Robert behind. But he didn't seem to get the hint. So, I tried to motion for him to stay as I walked through the gate, but he tried to follow. I knew I had to say something, as much as I didn't want to.

"Robert, they're not going to let you in," I said.

"Why not?" he asked, defensively. "Is it because of how I'm dressed. Because I've seen golf before. This would fit right in with what some of those guys wear."

"It has nothing to do with what you're wearing, even though a retarded, blind, quadriplegic boy could dress himself better. It's just that this is a really old fashioned and historic golf club. It has some rules that are a little dated."

"They're not going to let me in because I'm black? Really? So, you're telling me that if Tiger Woods showed up, you guys wouldn't let him play because he's black?"

"Technically, it's not because you're black," I said, ducking through the gate and watching him get stopped by the two guards. "It's because you're not white."

Chapter 11

As soon as I crossed the threshold of the gate, Robert Tindall was absent from my mind. I was calm and relaxed again. I strutted up to the doors of the clubhouse, confidence at my usual high, and walked in. To no surprise, my appearance did not garner much attention. I looked around the clubhouse, but did not see the man I knew as Gordon Stanton. I walked up to the bartender, who would know every member of the club.

"Do you know the name Gordon Stanton?" I asked.

"No, I don't, Mr. Alterson. Should I?" he asked.

"Maybe. I just thought I saw him here. He's a gray-haired guy with a thick mustache. Does that sound like anyone you know?"

"No," he said, skeptically. "Is something wrong?"

"No...no, no, no, nothing's wrong," I said, shaking my head. "I ran into him last weekend and couldn't remember where I knew him from. I thought it might be from the country club. Must be somewhere else."

I sat at the bar hoping the bartender would say something else, but he didn't. Then I saw him nervously glance at another group at the bar. I looked over at them, but did not see a reason for the bartender to feel nervous. It was just a group of a few club members, all of whom I recognized. The bartender continued to glance at them, and finally I understood what he was doing. I don't know how I didn't realize it when I first looked. One of the guys sitting at the bar was with Gordon Stanton at the country club last week. The bartender must have been trying to signal me.

Now that I had a lead, the question was: what should I do next? I needed to talk to the young, lanky man that sat with Gordon Stanton last week. And I needed to get him alone. But that didn't seem too likely when he was surrounded by that group. Then, suddenly, my instincts kicked in and I knew exactly what I had to do.

I made eye contact with the bartender and ordered a beer. I sat on one of the barstools just as the bartender finished pouring my beer. He set the drink in front of me and I feigned interest in a rerun of Sportscenter. I drank my beer without saying a word, hardly daring to look at the group on the other side of the bar, but keeping enough of an eye on them to make sure they didn't leave without me noticing. I ordered another one and continued to watch the television in silence, still keeping my eye on the group. When I finished that one, I ordered a third. Halfway through my third beer, they finally looked like they were ready to leave. I chugged a few gulps of beer so that it was nearly gone and the bartender walked over to me before the other group. Just like I knew he would.

"Did you want another beer, Mr. Alterson?"

"No, thanks."

"Okay. Should I just put this on your tab then?"

"*Actually*, I'd like to pay my tab today."

I handed him my card and the bartender walked to the register and printed out my tab. It had been about a month since I paid it last, and, though I didn't plan to pay my tab today, it was the perfect opportunity to pass a secret message.

I couldn't help but chuckle when the bartender set my tab in front of me. $14,384.64! Holy shit! Maybe I needed to cut back a little bit on the beers. Shock aside, I paid my tab and added a $4,500 tip. At the bottom of the receipt, I scribbled, *get me alone with him.*

I slowly sipped the rest of my beer as I stealthily watched the bartender address the group across from me. I couldn't hear exactly what he said, but he seemed to be explaining something and offering his apologies to the young, lanky man. The young man seemed to be taking whatever the bartender said in stride because he remained behind as his friends walked to the exit. When they were out the door, I walked over without wasting any time.

"Sam Alterson," I said, offering him my hand.

"Craig Showen," he replied, shaking my hand with a confused look on his face.

"I don't mean to intrude, but I've seen you around here a few times, so I thought I would take the opportunity to introduce myself."

That seemed to alleviate his concerns because he opened right up after I said that.

"Nonsense, you're not intruding at all. There was a problem with the machine, so I told my friends to head to the range and that I'd catch up."

"Technology. What a cruel, fickle bitch."

"Amen to that," he said, chuckling.

Just like that, I knew I had him. I knew I was good with the ladies, but I'd never tried to woo a man the same way. Turns out men are even easier than women. "Wanna grab a beer while we wait?" I asked, knowing the answer before he said it. The other members never missed a chance to rub elbows with the big shots at the club, and I'd certainly made a name for myself, winning the club tournament the previous year and by being...well...simply by being me.

"I don't see why not."

The bartender brought us each a beer, then walked back to the card machine and pretended to mess with it. He didn't seem to be able to solve his fake problem, so he walked to the backroom, shooting me a wink when Craig was looking the other direction.

"So, how long have you been a member here, Craig?"

"It's been about two years now. I'd been out a few times with one of the guys I was with earlier. The guy in the green shirt. Anyway, he invited me a few times and I got asked to join about six months later. How about you?"

"Shoot, it's been a little over five years now. I don't think I've missed my weekly round since my second year."

"I wish I could say the say the same, but work gets in the way sometimes."

"I don't know what you're talking about! I see you here almost every time I'm here. Where do you work at?"

Craig laughed. "To be fair, I did say sometimes. I'm actually the Chief of Surgery over at the general hospital. I've been there about three years now. Before that I worked in Los Angeles as a surgical resident. It was tough to leave, but the job here was just too good to pass up. I actually got my in at the hospital with a family friend. Maybe you've seen him here before. He's a muscular guy by the name of Darren Jotworth. He's on the board of the hospital and recommended me for the position. I've had him out five or six times this year. He's hoping to get invited to join himself."

I hardly listened as Craig finished. As soon as he mentioned Darren Jotworth, I was only focused on that. Because I knew who he was. He was with Craig and Gordon Stanton last week.

"Oh yeah, I think I saw him here a few weeks ago."

"Last week, actually."

"That's right. And who else was you with?"

"The other two were older guys. One of them is Frank Davacchio and the other guy is my dad, Dale Showen."

Frank Davacchio? So that was Gordon Stanton's real name. It felt good to know, yet it sounded strangely familiar. I knew I'd heard it before somewhere, but I don't know where.

"I thought there might have been someone you were related to."

"Yeah, dad was a Chief of Surgery too, until he retired ten years ago. And you might recognize Frank because he's running for Senate."

"That's it! That's where I know him from!" I genuinely exclaimed, though Craig had no idea for my ulterior motives. I knew I recognized the name. I saw it on a sign when I walked to the bar after the gym the previous week. I'd never seen him before, but I knew I saw the name.

"Frank's a friend of the family. He actually went to college with dad," Craig began. "Dad's even helping him with the campaign. Dad's having a party and Frank is going to stop by...might stop by ..." Craig caught himself revealing more than he should have in his efforts to impress me. Almost on cue, the bartender returned with Craig's receipt and sorted out the problem. Craig signed it and shook my hand again. I played it off as if I didn't hear anything and said goodbye, but it was too late. I was already beginning to think about the next step.

Chapter 12

"The guards here are really nice," Robert snidely remarked as I walked out the gates. "And how long were you in the there? Two hours? Don't worry about me out here. I'm homeless, so I don't mind waiting outside. Feel free to take all the time you need."

There he goes, right back at it. Right back to the fucking bitching. He couldn't even give me one minute to revel in the fact that I found a useful piece of information before he started that again? Of course not because that would actually make him tolerable to be around. But I decided to be the bigger man and chose not to acknowledge any of that.

"I know that took a while, but I found something."

"Something? What do you mean you found something?" he asked, almost sounding upset by my answer.

"I mean I found a piece of information that's gonna help us find out who's behind this. So the clubhouse was a success!" I said trying to encourage him.

"You found a piece of information. That doesn't help us. I want you to find out who wants me dead."

"That's how you figure out that kind of stuff. You find some information and it helps you learn more information and then you're able to figure out what's going on."

"Woohoo," he cheered, unenthusiastically as he began a sarcastic tirade. "I'm glad you found a piece of information. Now it's like a scavenger hunt. We find one piece of information and that leads us to another piece of information and so forth. And if we're really lucky, we'll be able to collect all the pieces and we'll win the scavenger hunt. The we'll win the prize of getting to meet the person who wants me dead! Doesn't that sound like fun?"

"Oh how silly of me to find something out? You've had the solution all along, haven't you? Oh, wait, that's right, you haven't had any answers. You haven't even had any ideas. You just sit on your ass complaining while I think of what we should do next. Maybe you should stop taking my hard work for granted and be grateful of the fact that I didn't put a bullet in your head the first time I saw you."

I wasn't going to let that obnoxious bastard put me in my place, and that shut him right up. Good. It was much more pleasant to walk in silence. Which is what we we did the entire distance back to the corner where I met him.

"So what now?" Robert asked, ruining the moment.

"We need to make some plans about what we're going to do..."

"What about at that hotel from last night? That would be a good place to make some plans," Robert interrupted.

"That place is pretty expensive. I'm not sure it makes sense to spend that money if it takes longer than we expect. Not to mention the fact that they told me they would charge me double if you set foot in any of the rooms. No, I was more thinking that place you stayed last night. Does it have a suite or something like that?"

He could not hide the disappointment in his voice as he said, "Yeah...they do."

"Great. Let's go there. You lead the way."

"What? I don't know the way."

"You were just there last night. How do you not know the way?"

"I wasn't really expecting to go back." Robert started to look through his journal. "Okay, it's this way."

Well, if he didn't have the intelligence to remember the location, at least he had enough common sense to write it down.

Robert led the way, heading northwest of the country club. At least he was headed in the right general direction.

He was so focused on whatever was written in his page that he didn't even have time to drive me insane. What a nice change of pace.

After more than twenty minutes and two miles of walking, Robert stopped. We stood in the parking lot of an abandoned building that I'd never seen before. It didn't take a genius to know that Robert was lost.

"Wow, this motel is really nice," I quipped. "They look like they've got a lot of amenities."

"It's gotta be around here somewhere."

"I wouldn't bet on it. In fact, I bet we're farther away than when we first started. Admit it, you don't have the slightest fucking clue where you're going."

Robert didn't reply.

"How fucking stupid are you?"

"Just pull it up on your phone. That'll be easiest," he said, strangely defensively.

I wasn't going to argue with him. I was sick of walking and even more sick of Robert. I pulled out my phone and searched for nearby motels. The closest one was just over a mile away.

"Is it called Rebates Motel?"

"I don't know," Robert said, maintaining his defensive tone.

"What do you mean you don't know? You just fucking spent the night there."

"Sorry I didn't take the time to remember the name," Robert replied, with no sincerity. "I told you, I didn't expect to ever return." Apparently that, along with the directions to the motel, hadn't made it into his journal.

I didn't even bother to reply to Robert, instead opting to lead the way to Rebates Motel. Serendipitously, the phone provided me an excuse to walk in silence again. Any time Robert seemed about to say something, I'd pretend to look at my phone to make sure that we were on the correct path. I, of course, chose to ignore how simple the route really was, not wanting to waste what I quickly recognized as a golden opportunity.

As soon as we walked into the motel, I regretted not getting a room at the hotel from the previous day. Or literally anywhere else. The hostess looked liked the Crypt Keeper's great grandmother. She had more wrinkles than corduroy pants. And she was about the best thing the place had going for it. The interior looked like it hadn't been updated since the early sixties (that's 1860's, mind you). And that was about the last time that it looked like it'd been cleaned, too. There were small pieces of food and other debris scattered across the floor, making it a challenge to take a step without hearing a crunch. Paint was chipping from all the walls and a thick layer of dust covered everything in the room, even the front desk.

"How can I help you?" the hostess asked. Frankly, I was surprised she even knew anyone was in the room. Her vision couldn't have been that good, though, because she didn't have even the slightest reaction to Robert's appearance.

"I'd like to book a room for a week. A suite, if you have one available." That was the charmer in me coming out again. I didn't really expect all the suites to be booked. There were only three cars in the parking lot for chrissakes. And I'm pretty sure that two of them were just parked there because it was a closer walk to the restaurant next door.

I paid for the full week up front in cash and the hostess gave us two keys. The room was exactly like what I expected it to be. Like the lobby, it looked as if it hadn't been updated in several decades. It was only slightly cleaner than the lobby, but you get what you pay for. One hundred dollars for one week only gets you so much service. Though, the low price did make me curious as to what Robert used the rest of my money for.

"Well, this seems like it'll...suffice." I walked around the room, exploring more of its intricacies. I quickly realized I was better off not knowing more and addressed Robert again. "I'll meet you back here tomorrow morning at eleven. We can talk about what we're gonna do next then." I turned to leave, but thought of one more thing to add. "Do what you want in the bedroom, so long as they let you keep staying here, but let's try to keep the main room looking decent. I don't want to see any of your weird, homeless-person collections or anything like that. And for the love of God, pants are not optional."

Chapter 13

The next day I arrived at the room at precisely eleven a.m. (yes, I can be on time when I choose to be). I was not surprised to find that Robert was nowhere to be found. And by that I mean that he was nowhere in the main room. He was probably jerking off. If I'd been homeless for as long as he was, I would be ecstatic just to have walls around me while I was going to town on myself. I'd be taking advantage of every second of that; it sure beats the alternative: putting on a show for everyone that walked by. Nonetheless, I had no desire to confirm my suspicions, choosing instead to remain blissfully ignorant.

Five minutes later, Robert walked out of his bedroom. "Took you long enough," I said, not bothering to hide my contempt.

"I'm...not good with clocks. You know, don't really have much of a need to use them," he said unconvincingly. So he was jerking it.

"Whatever, let's just get to work."

Robert and I sat at the table in the living room of the suite for nearly two hours, making very little headway. The homeless man was awfully high and mighty. Nothing I suggested was good enough for him. He, however, offered very few ideas, and the few that he did suggest were either utterly inane or destined to fail in seconds. When he wasn't shooting down one of my ideas or suggesting we "sneak in" on a hot air balloon (yes, that really was one of his ideas), Robert wrote in his journal. Still, he had the audacity to dismiss every one of my ideas. Finally, I couldn't take it any longer.

"I'm starving. Let's take a break and get some food." Truthfully, I wasn't hungry, but this was more an excuse so I didn't have to speak to him for a while.

"Yeah, I'm sure you really are starving. Food must *really* be hard to come by for you, what with how readily you hand out hundreds." It was no wonder someone wanted this bastard dead, and I was seriously considering completing a job for the first time in my career, but ultimately decided that Robert may somehow be useful to me.

"It's a fucking expression, but I'm not surprised it confuses you. You probably don't have a lot of opportunities to use them on the street." Again, that shut him up. It was remarkable how quickly a well-placed comeback could silence him. "I know this is kinda asking a lot, but does this place have room service?"

"Even if it did, you probably wouldn't want to eat it,." The statement was layered in condescension, but he was actually right, at least if the room was any indication of the quality of the food.

Like the lobby, paint chipped from each of the walls, none of which were the same shade of white. The carpet was a deep red, shaggier than any I'd seen. One of the table legs had been replaced with an old two-by-four, causing it to sit unevenly. None of the chairs surrounding it matched one another, nor the table. Judging by that, I would have been better off finding a piece of bark from a nearby tree and chewing on that to tide me over, rather than eating whatever this motel attempted to call food.

"I'll just go out and get us something," I said. "You...uh...stay here and hold down the fort."

"I can come with."

"Well, it's really just a one person job. Plus, this'll give you some time to think of new ideas."

I walked out the door before Robert had a chance to argue any further. There was a burger place a block away, and I returned with combo meals for both of us. Robert didn't thank me for the gesture. Not that this surprised me, as he didn't offer his thanks for anything I did for him. I only gave him two hundred dollars and a place to sleep. Oh, and I didn't kill him. Why should I expect him to be grateful?

When we finished the meals (Robert eating extraordinarily quickly for someone that was ungrateful and did not take hands outs), we continued our planning. The process was, if anything, more strenuous than the first attempt. His attempts to refute my ideas became so feeble that he lowered himself to simply rewording my plans and presenting them as his own. By the time the sun set, I begrudgingly agreed on a plan, mainly because I did not want to have to spend another second with Robert. I sensed that he felt the same way, but I couldn't have given a fuck less. I was just glad that I wouldn't see him again until the day of the party.

Chapter 14

Four days later, it was time to put the plan into action. I met Robert at the motel to go over one final run-through.

"I still don't see why I can't just come into the party with you right away." Leave it to him to start making objections just an hour before we were due to arrive.

"We went over this. Even if we did give you a decent haircut and trimmed your beard to a non-homeless level, there still isn't enough water on the planet to clean the dirt off you and wash away whatever odor you're emitting." Robert couldn't argue, mostly because even he knew that a truer statement had never been spoken.

First, we needed to rent a car. I knew that we would not be able to arrive at the party via taxi, nor was I going to allow Robert to ride in my Camaro. We had to keep up appearances, and that meant driving a car fitting of our - or rather, my - social status. The nearest car rental agency was less than a mile away, but that did not stop Robert from bitching the whole way.

"I can't believe we need to rent a car. I expected you to have a Bentley waiting for you in your garage," he said. I pretended not to hear him, as we'd already gone over this numerous times.

We got a car without an issue (a luxury I'd later wish I hadn't taken for granted) - a 2015 Lexus RC - and drove to the party. We rode in silence, save for the radio, which Robert insisted on controlling. I conceded this, simply for the fact that it would mean less of Robert talking. He surfed through the stations for a few minutes before becoming weirdly intrigued by opera music and stopping to listen to that. We could not have been more different.

The Showen estate was immaculate. It was a colossal pearly white, without a speck of dirt or dust. The shrubs and trees were perfectly maintained, the grass a luscious green, neatly trimmed. The back of the house no doubt contained a large swimming pool or some other ostentatious fixture. I would have thought it excessive and grandiose had I not remembered what my apartment looked like. You can call me a lot of things, but I am not a hypocrite.

By the grace of (insert your deity here, because I'm accepting of all forms of religious idiocy), Robert exited the car at precisely the right second. A valet approached to park my car. That was something I could get used to. He drove away as I walked to the door to enter the party.

No one in the party said anything as I walked through the door. In fact, no one gave me a second look. With my dapper appearance and charming smile, I fit right in. Next step: find Frank Davacchio.

That turned out to be a much easier task than I expected. He was, after all, a politician. He stuck out like a sore thumb, schmoozing everyone he talked to. No one was genuinely that much of an ass-kisser, pretending to care about the names of other people's dogs and which farmer's markets they bought their produce at. It was quite the spectacle. I had to stop myself from laughing on more than one occasion. I didn't want to look away, but I knew that I couldn't stare forever, so I began to mingle.

I could give Frank a run for his money when it came to talking to people. I would have made a fine politician myself if only I gave a damn about the livelihood of others.

It did not take Frank Davacchio long to spot me, either. He stood next to a beautiful woman and her husband, a fat, ugly bastard that must have been filthy rich to get a wife that hot.

Despite the fact that he was in the middle of a conversation, Davacchio couldn't help but continually glance at me. I knew what he was doing. He wanted to make sure that he didn't lose me. He wanted to talk to me. And that was exactly what I wanted, too.

When he finished his conversation, the Senate candidate made a beeline for me. "Fancy seeing you here," he said, trying to maintain his composure.

"I was going to say the same thing, *Gordon*." I said, defiantly, adding a little extra emphasis to the name. It gave me a maniacal sort of satisfaction to toy with him.

"What the hell are you doing here?" he asked. His tone changed immediately. He became defensive, worried even. And I loved every second.

"You could say I'm a friend of the family." Davacchio didn't have to reply for me to know that he didn't appreciate my answer. The veins on his forehead popped out so far they looked like they might explode. He clenched his fists so tightly I was certain his hands were going to break. For a moment, I thought that he was going to punch me, but I knew that he never would. Not in front of all these people.

"How the fuck did you get invited here?"

"Now, now, now, is that any way a candidate for Senate should talk?"

"Listen here, you son of a bitch, whatever it is you're trying pull, it's not going to work." He stormed away, but his fake, political smile returned in an instant.

"It looks like it already did," I added, before he was too far away. Davacchio didn't respond, but I knew he heard me.

I watched Davacchio as several people tried to approach him, but he brushed each of them off. He seemed polite, but I knew rage was filling him. He walked through the living room and into the kitchen. I followed him through there and watched as he walked upstairs. I tried to continue my pursuit, but lost Davacchio as I nearly ran into Craig Showen. I ducked out of the way at the last second. The last thing I wanted was to blow my cover now. He *technically* never invited me to the party.

I looped back around through the dining room, down a long hallway, and back to the stairs. I rushed up, trying not to waste any more time. There were three rooms: two to the left and one to the right of the stairs. I searched the two rooms on the left, but they were both empty. When I got to the third room, I had to do a double take at what I saw. Robert stood outside one of the large windows on a balcony. As soon as he saw me, he started to bang on the glass.

I ran to the window and threw open the window. "Shut the hell up! Do you want someone to hear you?"

"Relax. No one can hear me. I..." he started.

"What the hell are you even doing up here, anyway? Did you suffer a brain injury or are you just that stupid?"

"Will you just stop yelling at me and let me explain?"

"What possible explanation could you have?"

"I came here to try to find a way into the house," he began.

"That wasn't part of the plan," I interjected. "You had one task, one simple task: compile a list of license plates of all the cars. But you couldn't even fucking do that right."

"Will you just let me finish? Anyway, so I came up to try to find a way into the house." He paused to see if I would interrupt again. I wanted to, but I bit my tongue. "It became clear that all the windows were locked, though. I was about to climb down and see if I could find a way in on the ground, when I heard someone come in the room." He must have seen the contemptuous look on my face because he added, "I hid, so no one saw me. I'm sure of that. Two guys walked in and started yelling at each other."

"What did they look like?"

"They were both older guys. One had a mustache and the other had a beard." Frank Davacchio and Dale Showen. "I couldn't exactly hear what they were saying, but the mustached guy seemed pretty upset at the bearded guy. One of them grabbed a phone out of the nightstand and made a call. Then they both left. I'm surprised you didn't see them because they left right before you walked in."

So either Frank or Dale called someone? The question was: who? I needed to get my hands on that phone. I just had to hope they had the oversight to leave it in place.

Chapter 15

I didn't waste another moment talking. I ran to the nightstand like Mr. Sanders toward a free buffet. I pulled the drawer open so hard that it almost came off its tracks. I shuffled some papers and a cigar case with an insignia that looked vaguely familiar. And there, like a hot blonde in a sea full of South Carolina sixes, sat the phone. It was so surreal that I almost couldn't believe it. This might be the piece that finally put this whole mystery to rest.

"Let's get outta here," I said.

"Alright," Robert said, starting for the door.

"Not so fast. We're not going back through the party. I might get killed if they see me. I don't want to find out what they'd do if they see you."

"Down the balcony it is then."

Robert climbed through the window and I followed close behind. When we got to the balcony, it became clear to me that there were no stairs.

"How the hell are we supposed to get down?" I asked.

"We climb," Robert replied, in a matter-of-fact tone.

"Oh my mistake. I left my climbing gloves and grappling hook in the car."

Robert climbed over the railing and scaled down deftly. I climbed down much less gracefully - despite what James Bond films may portray, suits were not meant for those kind of moves. I lost my grip halfway down, falling to the ground, landing on my back. Robert wasn't the least bit concerned about my wellbeing. In fact, he laughed at the sight. I pulled myself up and we ran to the car, having to come up with a quick cover story to explain to the confused valet, a task I easily undertook. I squealed my tires as I hammered on the gas, leaving Frank, Dale, and the rest of the party behind.

When I got back to my apartment, I tried to get into the phone, but unsurprisingly discovered that it had a lock placed on it. It wasn't your typical fingerprint or passcode lock, either. No, it was encrypted in a way I'd never seen before. But that was no problem. I knew just the man for the job.

Chapter 16

The next day I dropped the phone off at Trevor's apartment. He said it would take a few days to get into the phone. Something about how the encryption was more difficult than any he'd ever seen and needing some sort of algorithm to unlock it. It all sounded like a bunch of bullshit computer gibberish to me. I may or may not have expressed that sentiment, which he in turn volleyed back by saying that it would take a few days longer than he initially estimated. I said something about shoving my foot so far up his ass that he'd taste the rubber from the sole of my shoes for month. I don't know, I don't remember all the details.

More than a week later, I still hadn't heard from Trevor. That wasn't like him. He always knew how to get ahold of me. And despite the fact that we had a *less than pleasant* interaction the last time we spoke, I knew Trevor wouldn't keep this kind of information from me.

I headed over to Robert's motel room to discuss the next part of the plan with him. I booked him another week in the same room. *Shockingly*, it was still available.

"Robert! Make yourself decent and get out here!" I called from the entryway of the suite. Apparently he and I had different definitions of "decent", because he walked out in an old sweat-stained t-shirt and fraying boxers, despite the fact it was late into the evening. The last time I slept in this late was in my twenties after a marathon sex session that carried into the next morning. "I appreciate all the effort you went through to get dressed, but we need to talk."

"Of course you want to talk. All you ever want to do is talk. Meanwhile, someone is trying to kill me. But sure. Let's talk."

It took all the willpower I could muster to ignore his comment. "I still haven't heard anything about the phone. Have any other ideas?"

"No, the phone's pretty much our best shot."

"Nothing else? No other leads or possible solutions?"

"I thought you were supposed to be the master at solving jigsaw puzzles, the guy who could follow the trail of breadcrumbs."

"You're right. I'll do this all by myself. You just kick back and do nothing. Never mind the fact that I'm paying for you to have a place to sleep and food to eat." I slammed the door behind me as I left.

I couldn't believe the nerve of Robert. Not that anything he ever did or said really surprised me. I just would have thought he might at least have the *slightest* inclination to find the person that wanted him dead. I sure know I would. Maybe that makes me the weird one.

I went back to Trevor's apartment and knocked on the door. It was the only thing I had to go on. After more than a minute, Trevor still had not answered. Maybe he was out buying more drugs.

I walked around to the back of his building. Luckily, he lived on the ground floor, so I'd be able to see in. Unfortunately, however, all the blinds were drawn. Maybe he really wasn't there. Yet, for some reason, I could not shake the feeling that something was wrong, that something more sinister was afoot.

Seeing I was out of options, I grabbed a large rock from the ground, looked around to be certain there were no onlookers, and threw the rock through the window. This was the one time that the neighborhood could play to my advantage. It could easily look like some thug broke in and robbed the place. And worst come worst, I could reimburse Trevor for the window. That had to be thirty dollars tops, right?

Once the window was broken, I cleared away as much of the broken glass as possible and climbed through the window. Apparently, suits weren't made for that either. That was the price you had to pay for style. High-priced suits were not resistant to dirt - or in this case tears because I wasn't able to clear all the glass out.

It didn't take long for me to realize that something was amiss in Trevor's apartment. It was a mess, much more so than usual. Aside from the trash and other random debris, it looked like the place had been ransacked. To the untrained eye, the difference would have been indistinguishable, but I was no untrained eye. The kitchen, which was usually neatly unorganized, was a complete disaster. The pots and pans in the sink had been thrown on the floor. There was nothing sitting on the couch and the trash on the floor had been scattered, so much so that it actually made it easier to walk through. Most striking of all, though, was Trevor's computer. That was his one pride and joy, the only thing he actually cared about. The keyboard hung off the desk, wires and cords were strewn about, and one of the monitors was missing. That was more than peculiar.

I walked through the living room and into a part of Trevor's apartment that I'd never explored. There was a hallway with two doors, one on the left and one on the right. The door on the left led to a bathroom. Aside from the filth and overwhelming odor, it checked out. The other door led to a bedroom. What I saw almost made me vomit.

I like to think I have a pretty high tolerance for that kind of stuff, but this was like nothing I'd ever seen before. There was blood everywhere. And the smell the room emitted made the bathroom smell like wet pussy on a Saturday night. It smelled worse than Robert's feet the first time he took his socks off in front of me, which was quite the feat considering I'd remarked then that it smelled like a dirty diaper basking in the sun on a hundred degree day mixed with wet and dirty laundry that hadn't been cleaned since the days of Moses. Nothing I tried was strong enough to prevent the vile odor from wafting into my nostrils. My shirt and suitcoat were futile. A half-empty fast food bag couldn't counteract the smell. Even the surgical masks I found under Trevor's kitchen sink were powerless (you could always count on finding the weirdest shit in a drug addict's house). Alas, I decided to hold my breath and enter the room. I crossed the threshold of the door, preparing myself for whatever I might find.

If the evidence of a break in had not been obvious in my examination of the rest of the house, it became abundantly so as I examined the bedroom. The entire room was torn apart. The sheets laid on the floor in a crumpled mess and most of the clothes from the closet were strewn haphazardly throughout the room. The walls were covered in several large dents and bloody handprints. Clearly a struggle had taken place. Worst of all, there was blood everywhere. All over the bed, the closet, the nightstand, the carpet, the walls, and some even dripped from the ceiling. There was so much blood, more than I thought could be inside one human being. I walked around to the other side of the bed and that was when I saw it.

Trevor laid on his stomach next to the bed. I rolled him over. I'm not even really sure why. I already knew he was dead. What I saw, though, was so much worse than I could have imagined. His face was mangled to the point that he was nearly unrecognizable. It was beaten to a pulp. And it looked as though he'd been tortured. Most of his fingernails were ripped off and several of his fingers and toes had been reduced to stubs. There was really no telling what the fatal blow was; his body was covered in so many wounds and gashes it could have been any of them.

I couldn't look at him any longer. I never gave two shits about Trevor, but I never wanted something like that to happen to him. I walked out of the apartment in complete disbelief, shaken up, and unable to truly process the gravity of what I'd just seen.

Chapter 17

"Robert! Get your poor ass out of bed!" I yelled.

I ran to the hotel straightaway from leaving Trevor's place. The trip had given me time to process the information. Trevor was dead. That left me with no path forward, which is why I begrudgingly reached the decision to pay Robert an unprecedented second visit of the day.

"Julian, what the hell do want? What time is it?" he said as I opened the unlocked door. It came as no surprise to see that he had his head down, jotting in his journal.

"Get out of bed. We need to talk."

I walked back to the common area. Robert joined me a few minutes later wearing a dirty pair of tighty whitey underpants and a badly stained wife beater. Abiding by social norms was not his strong point. Nor was following simple and reasonable ground rules.

"What's so important that you needed to barge in here in the middle of the night?" Robert asked. He was awake for a few hours and he was really going to complain about not getting enough sleep?

"Trevor's dead," I replied.

"So, some guy I don't know is dead? That couldn't wait until the morning?"

"Trevor was the guy I brought the phone to last week. I don't know how they found out, but they did."

Robert paused for a moment, taking in what I said, seemingly trying to choose his words carefully. "Did you touch his body?" Not at all what I expected.

"What kind of fucked up question is that?" I asked.

"I'm serious. Did you touch his body or anything else in the apartment?"

"Well, seeing as I'm not a wizard and I'm not a ghost and I can't float, there's a strong possibility that I did touch some stuff in the apartment."

"You're an idiot," Robert said.

"Really? I'm the idiot?"

Robert started at me, stunned. "Are you stupid or just fucking arrogant?"

"You're the one asking these pointless questions."

"Pointless?! Don't tell me you're that stupid. If someone is dead, there's going to be an investigation. The police are going to be involved. And that place is literally crawling with your DNA. They're going to be after you in no time. I'd be surprised if they weren't waiting at your place as we speak."

It was a good point and something I hadn't thought of. Sure, I did a good job concealing my identity from the people I conned, but I'd never needed to do that from the police. I'd never feared retaliation or police involvement because implicating me would only do the same for my accuser. I still had fingerprints, still had trails of myself that could be found, if anyone knew where to look.

Yet, that was not what Robert dwelled on. He quickly shifted the conversation in a different direction. "None of this makes sense," he said.

"What do you mean? It makes perfect sense," I replied.

"Think about it. Why would they go through all the trouble of finding you and paying you if they were so willing to kill? Why didn't they just kill me if it was so easy for them?"

As much as I hated to admit it, Robert had a point. The reason people hired me, the reason they hired hitmen in general was because they didn't want the blood of another on their hands. They wanted to mitigate some of the culpability. But that wasn't the case with these guys. They proved that murder was just an afterthought to them. They cast away the life of an innocent man - or at least as innocent as junkie hacker could be - without the blink of an eye. Robert was right. There was more to the puzzle.

I had not said a word in a considerable amount of time, something Robert obviously took note of. "What's the matter, were the thoughts of a lowly homeless man too complicated for you to follow?"

Ah, back to the snide remarks that I missed so much. "No, I was more dumbfounded that you could actually put together a logical, coherent sentence," I retorted without missing a beat.

"But it was logical?"

"Yes," I said, shaking my head. I couldn't believe that was the point he focused on. "Now let's talk about what actually matters. Why do you think that they didn't just kill you?"

"I have no idea."

"Stroke of genius ran out that fast, huh?"

"You're supposed to be the smart one here. What's your bright idea?"

"Maybe they don't actually want you dead."

"Then why would they have hired a hitman?"

"They didn't."

"Yes, they did."

"No, they didn't."

"They hired you," he said, confused.

"But I don't kill people."

"What do you mean you don't kill people?"

"I mean I don't kill people. It's pretty fucking self-explanatory."

"I don't get it. Why would they have hired you to kill me if you don't kill people."

"It's complicated."

Robert pretended to check an imaginary watch. "Looks like I have plenty of time. Explain."

"I'm not a hitman, okay? I just give people the impression that I am a hitman so that they pay me to kill someone. And then when I don't, I blackmail them into keeping their mouth shut."

Robert paused for a few moments to take the information in. I can't imagine he'd ever heard of anyone in my line of work. I surely never had since I came up with the idea. When Robert finally did react, he did not speak. He looked at me with a mixture of contempt and disapproval. Apparently hitmen were okay in his books, but conmen who masqueraded as hitmen were not. The look, however, was short lived.

"So why did they hire you then?"

I thought about the question for a brief moment, but the answer came quicker than I expected. "Because they wanted us to meet."

"Why would they want that?"

"That's what we need to figure out."

Robert looked as if he was going to reply, but stopped. As the sound of police sirens approached, his ears perked up. He got out of bed and started to get dressed. "We need to go to Trevor's house. Now."

"Why?"

"I told you earlier. Police investigate murders. We need to get over there and get rid of any evidence of you ever being there."

I followed Robert to the door. He moved so quickly that he nearly shut it directly on my face. Fortunately, I caught it with my hand and began the trek.

On the walk, I thought not of Trevor, not of the people behind this, not even of the police, but of Robert. Each day I spent with him, he grew more enigmatic. I was weary of him from the start, of how someone so functional and cognitive could be homeless. Yet, he continued to surprise me, at times even outsmarting me. As certain as I was that there was more to the reason I was hired for this murder, I was beginning to think there was more to Robert as well.

Forgetting that it was locked, I led Robert to Trevor's front door. An eerie feeling swept over me, and the fact that the front door was slightly cracked open did nothing to wash that feeling away. Even before I could see into the apartment, I could feel that something was wrong.

The apartment was a shell of what it had been in my many trips there. The empty fast food bags and debris were all gone, the floor clean. The kitchen was clean, too. The pots and pans that littered the sink were gone. I opened the cupboards and each was empty. There was not a sign that anyone had ever been there.

I walked out of the kitchen and back to the living room. I looked through it to the table with Trevor's computers, at least where they should have been. But they weren't there. The table was clean. I could not fathom what happened. I was just in the apartment an hour ago. It had been a disaster. It didn't make sense.

I ran from the living room to the bedroom, Robert at my heels.

The once blood-stained walls were freshly painted. There was no sign of struggle, no sign of the brutal murder that had taken place. I crossed the room in two strides to the side of the bed, to the place where I found Trevor's body. I closed my eyes as I waited to see what lay there. But I knew the answer before I opened my eyes. Trevor's body was gone.

Chapter 18

I left Trevor's apartment with more questions than I had before entering. I knew I was dealing with some pretty well-connected, informed people. They had to be if they were able to track me down. But this was a whole other level. I knew it had to be them. There's no way the police would clean out a place that fast. They had official investigations and protocol to go through. The apartment would have been littered with cops if the police were involved. And there's no way the body would have been moved. Not that fast. No, these people were serious. They meant business.

Robert and I hightailed our asses out of the apartment as soon as it became clear that Trevor wasn't there. We reached the street corner where I first saw Robert and parted ways,

Robert turning right and me turning left back to my apartment.

Now, I don't pretend to be a harder motherfucker than I really am. I went back to my apartment scared shitless that night. It wasn't that I was scared that I might be next. I wasn't scared of my death. I really wasn't. In truth, I died sixteen years ago, as far as I was really concerned. No, I was scared because I didn't know what they would do, scared because I had no idea what was going to happen next. If they wanted me dead, I would be dead. They had proven that killing wasn't their main prerogative. I was scared because I had no idea why I was still alive, no idea what they wanted from me. It was the unknown that terrified me the most.

That night was a night unlike any other I'd spent in my apartment. The wind howled outside my window, but that was nothing new. The wind always blew. Darkness descended, engulfing the city in complete blackness, the likes of which hadn't been seen in recent memory. It was a new moon, so there was almost no light, aside from the street lights which somehow seemed dimmer than usual. And for the first time in my life I felt alone. Completely alone.

It was one of the worst nights of sleep that I can ever remember. I tossed and turned in my bed, waking up every ten or fifteen minutes. Every car that drove by, every creak of the floorboards, every cricket's chirp woke me up. And I could not shake the feeling that someone was watching me. Despite the fact that I lived on the top floor of my building, I felt like someone was outside my window. I even went so far as to scour my apartment, but, of course, I couldn't find anyone else. My paranoia was at an all-time high.

The next morning, I awoke to something unusual - an incoming call on my business phone. I had never received a call on that phone before. Trevor secured me a line that was blocked when making calls and completely untraceable. Of course, if this experience had taught me anything, it was to expect the unexpected. Begrudgingly, I answered.

"Hello."

"Julian," the voice on the other end said. It didn't long for me to identify the voice of Frank Davacchio. "I take it you got our little message last night."

I did not respond.

"I'll take your silence to mean that you did. I hope that spurred you on to complete your task."

"Fuck you."

Davacchio laughed. "I was hoping you would say that. Check your texts," he said, hanging up without another word.

When Davacchio hung up, I looked through my phone and saw that I had a message from a blocked number I did not recognize. I wasn't really much of a texter. If it didn't involve naked women, I wasn't interested. Something told me that wasn't what I would find. I opened the message. What I saw made my stomach churn and my heart break. I slammed my phone on the ground, smashing it to smithereens, anger billowing from my every pore. My sister sat on a chair, hands tied behind her back, held captive by Frank Davacchio and Dale Showen.

Like the rest of my personal life, I never talked about my sister, Courtney. I didn't think anyone knew she existed. She lived in central Georgia, and though we were only separated by a few hundred miles, we hadn't seen each other in more than five years. When we were growing up, we didn't see eye to eye. We fought like...well, brother and sister. But, as we got older and matured, we grew closer. Over time, life led us in different directions and we slowly drifted apart. We still talked every other month or so, but that was more out of obligation than anything else. Our conversations had become superficial, never scratching beneath the surface. I didn't even know what she did for work, and she she sure as hell didn't know what I did. Despite all that, she was the only person I truly cared about. I don't know how Davacchio or Showen or whoever was behind all this found out about her, but he did. They'd found my one weakness, and for that, they would pay. I would stop at nothing until I hunted them all down and freed my sister.

Chapter 19

Newly motivated, I met up with Robert later that day. Out of answers and with a lack of other options, we needed to be proactive. If the answers didn't come to us, then we needed to go out there and find them ourselves. So we went to the one place that held nothing but answers.

Robert and I walked up the long flight of steps to our destination. It was an old building, one of the oldest in the entire city. Built in the 1800's, it was decrepit now. It was badly in need of a renovation. But, as much as I hated politicians, I had to side with them for choosing not to take action in this case.

"I still don't understand why we're going here," Robert said.

"We've been through this," I replied.

"Don't you have a computer at your house?" he asked.

"Yes," I answered.

"Why don't we just go there?"

"Because the *last* thing I could possibly want is for you to know where I live."

"Couldn't we just buy a couple and go to a coffee shop or something then?"

"No. Not an option," I said.

"Why not?"

"Because I'm not your personal fucking ATM."

"Well surely you can afford it."

"Of course I can afford it," I said. "I can also afford to buy you a new house and pay for it for the rest of your life, but I'm not going to do that either. So here we are."

I held the door open and followed Robert into the public library. We walked past an old librarian. She looked like she was two days away from the graveyard, yet the scowl she wore would have sent shivers down the spine of even the toughest man. If I didn't think that the mere force of my breath could send her to the grave early, I might have been scared. So we continued on, hardly giving her a second look. We stopped at a cluster of computers and sat down.

"Alright. Let's start with what we know," I said.

"Shh," Robert said, angrily.

"What?" I asked, concerned that he might have seen or heard something.

"This is a library. You're supposed to be quiet."

"That's only in the TV shows. Real libraries aren't like that. You can practically yell in here and no one will do anything." Then, to top it off, I did just that. "LOOK AT ME! I'M YELLING IN A LIBRARY! WHO'S GOING TO DO ANYTHING ABOUT THAT?" I was about to stand on top of my chair and continue, but, before I could, I was stopped.

"QUIET!" a voice screamed, in an ear-splittingly loud level. I looked over my shoulder and saw that it was the old librarian with a large megaphone in her hand. Apparently she didn't see the irony in using a megaphone to quiet me.

"See, I told you," Robert said in a whisper.

"Okay, but to be fair, I was yelling," I said, at my normal speaking volume. "She's not going to do anything if I just talk like this." Wrong again.

"DO I NEED TO TURN THIS THING UP LOUDER? I SAID BE QUIET!" the librarian yelled in response.

"That old bat has ears like a...well, a bat," I said in a lower voice, still refusing to whisper. Apparently that still wasn't enough.

"YOU CAN EITHER BE QUIET OR I CAN SHOVE THIS MEGAPHONE DOWN YOUR THROAT AND HIT YOU OVER THE HEAD WITH MY CANE A FEW TIMES. THAT OUGHTA KNOCK SOME SENSE INTO YOU!" She wielded her cane with surprising dexterity. I had to admit, she was becoming a little bit intimidating.

"See," Robert said, still in a whisper.

"So let's start with what we know," I said, now talking in a whisper. I could see Robert grinning to himself, so I shot him a look. The grin immediately disappeared.

As always, Robert had his face in his little diary or journal or whatever the fuck he called it. "Well we know that Dale Showen and Frank Davacchio aka Gordon Stanton are involved. Both men seem to be working for someone else. Seeing as Frank Davacchio is a candidate for Senate, it would seem to reason that whoever they're working for is a pretty powerful person. Dale is a retired surgeon. And we don't know a whole lot else about Frank/Gordon."

"Let's start there," I said.

I turned to my computer, hoping that Google would be able to provide some answers. I started by simply searching Frank Davacchio's name. Since he was a political candidate - and one of considerable notoriety, as I was beginning to find out - there was quite a bit of information out there about him. He had an MBA in Accounting & Finance and a law degree from Stanford. The hopeful future Senator was widowed about ten years ago and remarried. Davacchio's new wife was barely half his age. He had three kids, each with his first wife. It looked as though he had been a pretty successful trial lawyer before being appointed Attorney General for the State of Florida. That was the stepping stone to his political career because he joined the state House of

Representatives shortly thereafter. I read page after page. There certainly was not a lack of information about Frank Davacchio. I just didn't know how any of it was going to help us figure out who the puppet master of this twisted marionette show was. I turned to Robert to see if he might have been able to gather any leads, but his screen was blank, still sitting on the Google homepage.

"What the hell have you been doing?" I asked. "Just watching me?" I was careful not to raise my voice above a whisper.

"You seem like you've been doing a pretty good job of gathering information," he said.

"I have. And this process would go a hell of a lot faster if you decided that you actually wanted to contribute."

"Yeah," he said, nervously, almost embarrassed.

"You do know how to use a computer?" I asked, almost kicking myself for asking such a stupid question. Robert did not answer. "Let me teach you," I said, feigning kindness. "See what you do is take your fingers - those are those little dangly things that are attached to your hands - and use those to press the buttons on the board in front of you, you know the squiggly little characters. Those are called letters. If you type them in the correct order, sometimes they make a word. So what we do is we take those words and enter them into Google. That's that little thing right in front of your face. See how it says G-O-O-G-L-E? Google! And sometimes it can be helpful to type a couple of words or even a phrase. Now that's pretty tricky, so let me give you an example. You could try something like 'Frank Davacchio Senate' or 'Frank Davacchio Associates'. Then you click on any links that seem interesting - those are those blue things that pop up when you enter your search. Now you try."

Robert seemed angry, but he did so nonetheless. Apparently my first hunch had been correct because he struggled to type even simple phrases into Google. I tried not lose my patience too much as I helped him, but it felt like I was teaching a kindergartener how to use a computer for the first time. It was such a strange gap in knowledge for someone that came across so intelligent in other areas.

When Robert finally got the hang of it - which took an amount of time that I do not care to say - we continued our search. Having exhausted almost all the information on Frank Davacchio, I decided to turn my attention to Dale Showen. Unfortunately, Dale was not nearly as well-known as Frank, so information about him was harder to come by. There was no biography, no information about schools he attended or his family, just a few mentions of him in medical journals and several articles about successful surgeries he'd completed. Really nothing that would benefit us, even less so than what I found about Frank. I tried searching both of their names together, but that didn't return any results, either. I turned to Robert, hoping that *somehow* he'd been able to find a crucial piece of information. Boy was that an optimistic thought.

Robert had somehow managed to exit out of Google and open Microsoft Word. He had been typing phrase after phrase and pressing enter, each time sending him down a line. He seemed confused about why he wasn't generating any results, but remained undeterred. He determinedly gave it his best effort. I could not help but chuckle, and nearly fell out of my chair laughing when I saw that he had been doing this for more than twenty pages.

"You know what, Robert," I said, "maybe you should take a break. I'll take over the search for a little bit."

"I have to take a piss anyway," Robert grumbled. I don't know if he actually did or if he just felt embarrassed by his lack of contributions. Regardless, I didn't mind to see him go. It was starting to distract me from the task at hand.

I exited out of Microsoft Word on Robert's computer, wanting desperately to save the document to laugh at it another time, but ultimately decided against it. I reopened Google for him on the off chance that he gathered the courage to try again. Then, I went back to my computer and continued my search.

There had to be something I was missing, some piece of the puzzle, something to help me connect the dots, but I could not for the life of me think of what. I tried every phrase, name, and idea I could possibly think of, in every combination. Yet, still I yielded no meaningful results. We were no further than when we first walked into the library. I pounded my keyboard in frustration, but quickly realized the mistake in my actions. I looked over my shoulder and saw the librarian glaring at me. Apparently, pounding the keyboard was frowned upon, but it wasn't *nearly* the unforgivable sin that talking was. That was when Robert returned from the bathroom.

"You ready to give it another shot, big guy?" I asked, continuing to mock him.

"Yes" Robert said, a devilish grin spreading across his face. If I had been in his shoes, I never would have wanted to touch another computer again. I would have been completely turned off by the idea. But I'm not sure he knew he was doing anything wrong. For all I knew, Robert thought he was doing a good job.

We worked in silence before Robert finally spoke.

"I found something!" he said, as loud as a whisper could possibly be. It was louder, in fact, than when I talked in my normal register. The librarian, however, did not look over. The facade of a whisper was enough for her. I hated librarians.

"What did you find?" I asked, trying my best not to loathe the librarian.

"It's an old picture of Dale and Frank. And there's another person with them!"

It certainly was an old picture. The boys looked to be no older than ten, yet there was no mistaking Dale Showen and Frank Davacchio. Even in their youth, they bore most of the same facial features. I would have bet a million dollars it was them. The real question was: who was the third boy? And was that person even important?

"Do you really think this is going to help us?" I asked, skeptically.

"Of course it's going to be helpful," he said, defiantly.

"Look at them, Robert. They're just boys. How's that supposed to help us? That must have been, what, forty, fifty years ago?"

"True, but if Dale and Frank have remained friends that long, who's to say that the third boy isn't still friends with them, too?"

"Kids drift apart from friends all the time. You're the perfect example. There's no way you're still friends with all the same people you were when you were ten."

"They do, but what if these three didn't? What if they're still friends to this day? Besides, it's not like we have a lot else to go off of."

"Okay fine, let's pretend for a second like this third boy is important. Who is he? Let's research him and see what we can find."

"I don't know," Robert said. "It doesn't say."

"Let me take a look at it." I pushed Robert's chair away and scooted mine in front of the computer. I tried to click the link on the picture to take me to the original website, but the access was restricted to school alumni. It was protected by a username and password, two things I definitely did not have. If only Trevor were still here. I always assumed he'd OD one day, but I never thought I'd miss him. Scratch that. I didn't miss him, I just needed his help. I went back to the picture and saw there was a caption: *photo taken by Alex Bellavick, sixth grader.* Maybe if we could track him down, we'd be able to figure out who the third person was. But would that really help us, or were we just grasping at straws?

"What do you think, Robert? Do you think we should try to find Alex Bellavick?"

"We have to. It's the only way we'll know for sure. And it's the only real lead we have." He hadn't made a snide remark since we found the picture, a sign that he might actually be sincere.

"You don't think it's going to be a dead end?"

"No. I mean, I don't know, but what else do we have to go off of?" It was true. It was the only useful piece of real information that we'd found all day. "What do we have to lose? Bellavick can't be a terribly common last name. How hard can it be to track him down?"

We searched the online phone directories and found a hit for Alex Bellavick in less than a minute. There was only one. Luckily for us, he lived less than two hours away.

"That settles it," Robert said. "We have to go talk to him."

"Alright," I said, "we can leave tomorrow." I was still skeptical. But Robert was right. What did we really have to lose? It couldn't hurt to look for him. The worst that could happen would be that we would lose a few hours of our time. And as far as I was concerned, a few hours wasted were still a few hours that we didn't spend ending up like Trevor.

Chapter 20

I walked to the public bus station the next morning, the second most loathsome and vile place on earth. I figured since I stepped foot in the first (the public library) the previous day that I might as well go to the second too, because I hate myself for some reason. Okay, that's not true. In actuality, I needed to get a rental car to drive us to Alex Bellavick's house and the agency I previously used was booked, leaving the bus as the only way I could get to the next closest agency.

My assumptions about public transportation were proven correct within minutes of boarding. I had to dodge vomit from a mutant hell-spawn (small child), a dog urinated on three consecutive seats as its owner scratched its back and said, "good boy", and one man smelled so pungent that he literally emitted waves of odor as if he were were a real life Pig-Pen. And that was all in the first third of the bus. I did not care to find out what other treasures lurked on the rest of the bus, so I grabbed a seat to myself and gave off a look that plainly said, "don't fuck with me or I *will* kill you". Not the kind of look that the douchebag 'tough guy' from the gym gives, but the kind that worried parents enough to avert their children's eyes from me.

The rest of the bus ride went by uneventfully. I pulled the cord when the bus neared my stop and I exited without as much as a glance at any of my fellow passengers. I felt some of their stares and heard a few hushed whispers, the exact reactions I anticipated and craved.

I walked up to the car rental agency and through the doors. It was not a chain company, so it's name was a cheesy attempt at a pun. It was so pitifully idiotic that it pains me to think about, so much so that I have no desire to repeat it.

The line was completely empty. In fact, it looked as if no other person dared to step foot in the place, except for the few employees it somehow managed to pay. The clerk was a young kid, probably in his early twenties, with short brown hair and glasses that were much too large for his face. He wore a blissful grin, the kind filled with an ignorant sense of optimism. The harsh realities of the real world had not yet dawned upon him, but they would one day.

"How can I help you?" he asked, somehow able to maintain the smile with each word.

"I'd like to rent a car," I replied. What did he think I was there for? A routine bypass?

"Great. What's the name on the reservation?"

"Reservation? I don't have a reservation."

"I'm sorry, sir, but we've been booked for weeks."

"What do you mean you've been booked for weeks? This is a car rental agency. Your only job is to give people cars."

"You can't expect to rent a car on a holiday weekend without making a reservation. That's just poor planning."

"First of all, I'm not a visitor. I live here. Second of all, when I go to Subway, I expect them to make me a fucking sandwich, just like when I want a car, I expect to be able to rent one." My logic was sound, but he wasn't buying it.

"Then you should know how important it is to make a reservation. What are you gonna do next? Show up to the Super Bowl without a ticket and expect to get a seat?" The little shit clearly did not know that I did not have a tolerance for sarcasm unless I was on the delivering end. Still, I kept my cool. That was the only way I was going to be able to get what I wanted.

"That's a very funny joke. I understand if there's nothing you can do, though. I'd be glad to take my business to one of your competitors."

126

"You're more than welcome to try that, but I'd guess you're going to run into the same results everywhere else. The city surely is not in a shortage of people that want to rent cars." Alright then. On to Plan B.

I took a wad of cash out of my pocket and started counting bills. "What's it going to take? Two hundred dollars?" I laid two crisp one hundred bills on the counter in front of him, but he did not react. I laid another bill on the counter. "Three hundred?" Still nothing. I laid two more one hundred bills on the table. "Five hundred?" This time, he grabbed the cash and put it in his pocket.

"I'm sorry, sir, but there's nothing I can do."

"Then why the hell did you put the money in your pocket?"

"You put the money on the counter willingly. You gave it to me. Therefore, in the eyes of the law, it qualifies as a gift." I had no idea if what he said was accurate, nor did I care enough about the money to argue with him. I just wanted a damn car.

"Clearly you're not going to be able to do anything. Is your manager here? I'd like to speak with him."

I saw a coworker hurriedly approach the clerk. They had a hushed conversation for a few seconds, then the clerk's face lit up, somehow in a bigger grin. "On second thought, we may have something for you after all."

"So you were holding out on me, you bastard."

"Not exactly. We haven't been able to rent this one out since the incident, but you don't seem to be too picky. Follow me."

The clerk walked around the counter and through a door that presumably led to the car lot. We walked past several rows of cars until we came across one sitting alone. It immediately became clear why it was an afterthought. The Flintstones' car would have been more practical.

The car they agreed to rent me was an old Honda Accord, probably the first one ever made. The body of the car was white, but all four doors, the trunk, and the hood had been replaced, each in a different color. To an outsider, the rust would not have been noticeable, but when I took a closer look, it became clear that the rust had been painted over on each panel. Which brought one major question to the forefront of my mind: why was each panel replaced in a different color if it was all covered in rust? However, I did not want to test my luck, so I did not ask any more questions.

"I'll take it," I said, hardly pausing to consider the situation. Admittedly, I was desperate to get a car. Had I not been in such a situation, there's not one fucking chance in hell that I would have been caught dead in that piece of shit. That should have been enough to tell me that no good could come of renting the car.

Still, I gathered my courage and took the car to Robert's motel. I honked the horn four times before he came out of the room. Little did I know that the engine roared so loudly that the horn could not be heard and Robert only walked out on a mere whim.

We drove for less than twenty miles before the gas gauge lit up. *What the fuck*, I thought as I pulled into the nearest gas station. Begrudgingly, I began to fuel the car as Robert waited inside. I wasn't outside the car for more than a few minutes, but by the time I filled the tank, Robert was asleep in the passenger's seat. Between doing nothing and sitting on his ass in the motel room that I graciously paid for, Robert somehow must not have been able to find enough free time to get a good night's sleep.

I pulled out of the gas station parking lot and back onto the highway. As soon as we left the city, I was reminded once again about why I hated driving. There was nothing but fields and grass for miles. That and cows, but the only things they ever did were eat and shit. I'd never seen as much shit as I did in those first ten miles outside the city. To be quite honest, the sheer quantity was remarkable.

We hadn't gone more than twenty more miles before the gas light flashed again. There was no way the tank could be empty again. I was sure to completely fill it, adding just over fifteen gallons. There had to be something wrong with the gauge. I pulled my phone out and called the number that the clerk gave me.

"Hello," a voice on the other end of the phone said, instantly recognizable as the clerk that helped me.

"Yeah, hi, I just rented a piece of shit car from you guys and I've already had to put gas in it once and the gas light is flashing again. Don't you guys fill up the tank before renting out the cars?"

"Oh yes, that's part of our policy. No car is rented without a full tank of gas. I even personally made sure that the car we rented to you had gas in it before you left," he replied.

"Then there must be something wrong with the gauge because there's no way I've run out of gas twice in less than forty miles."

"There are a lot of problems with the car, sir, but I can assure you that there is nothing wrong with the gas gauge."

My patience was beginning to wear thin. First, they rent me a fucking junker that wouldn't even be fit for Robert. Then the clerk has the audacity to tell me the tank was full when I got it and there's no problem with the gas gauge. My anger was boiling over, but I did my best to contain it.

"I don't know what fucking planet you were born on, but here on Earth whatever the hell is going on with this car is called a fucking problem. Are you really going to stand there and tell me that that fucking rust bucket doesn't have any problems?" Like I said, I tried my best. And for me, that was actually pretty tame.

"Actually, I'm sitting," he said, pausing to laugh at his elementary joke. I remained silent. The clerk must have realized his error because he quickly moved on. "However, I never said the car had no problems. The car has lots of problems. I told you there was an incident. That's why we've never been able to rent it out before. I just said that there are no problems with the gas gauge, and I stand by that."

"Then why the hell is it lit up?"

"I'd guess because you need to get gas." He was lucky he wasn't standing in front of me, because I'd never felt a stronger urge to deliver a right hook.

"Thank you for your *brilliant* insight," I replied, "but how is that possible? I just told you that I filled up the tank less than twenty miles ago."

He paused for a moment, to consider my comment. "That sounds about right."

"Right? What are you fucking talking about?"

"I told you the car had some problems, so I'd say the reason you need to get gas again is due to a combination of putridly low gas mileage and a leaking gas tank."

I hung up the phone without saying another word, not wanting to break a second phone out of frustration. I pulled over at the nearest exit to fill the tank. That must have been the magic signal because Robert stirred in his seat. He stretched his arms and legs, but his head was still rested between the window and the seat.

"Finally there?" he asked, not bothering to open his eyes and look for himself. That would have required doing something, which was clearly against his fundamental beliefs. My usually low tolerance for Robert had completely evaporated thanks to that piece of shit clerk from the car rental agency.

"Yup, this is it. We've arrived in good old Bumfuck, Nowhere."

Robert opened his eyes to see for himself, whether he didn't see through the sarcasm or because he wanted to get a glimpse of the sight in front of us, I don't know. Regardless of the reason, he was in for a treat.

There were not a lot options of gas stations for me stop at. As a matter of fact, there were no other options. If I had even the slightest inkling that there was another gas station within five miles, I would have tried my luck, but something told me it was either this or run out of gas. And to be honest, the latter would have been the more appealing option if I had not already pulled into the gas station parking lot.

The lot was completely covered in gravel. No pavement. The pumps were beneath even the standards of those rust mongers on American Pickers. Needless to say, there was no credit card reader at the pump. That was the least of my concerns, though. I had more than enough cash to pay for the gas. Hell, I probably had enough money in my pocket to purchase the place if I had been so inclined. Fortunately, my doctor had elected to pass on the lobotomy, so a thought that certifiably insane would never seriously cross my mind.

When the tank was full, I walked inside to pay. The inbred hicks that operated the place looked like they'd never seen a hundred dollar bill before, but they accepted the money without a second thought. I could have laid a thousand dollar bill on the table and those buffoons wouldn't have known any better. Hell, I probably could have paid in monopoly money and they wouldn't have known the difference. Unfortunately, I'd left my monopoly billfold back at my apartment, so real cash was my only option.

I got back in the car and saw that Robert was beginning to stir. "Hey there, sleepyhead. Finally up from your little nappy poo?" Robert must have been too groggy to comprehend that I was mocking him because he did not acknowledge my comment.

"Are we there yet?" he asked, not bothering to open his eyes.

"I hate to break it to you, but we're still in the same gas station parking lot. But I can understand why you'd think we might be there, seeing as you've been asleep for the entire drive."

"Wake me up when we get there," he said in a daze. He was already beginning to fall back asleep.

"Yeah, I'll be sure to do that," I replied, sarcastically. I knew my comment fell on deaf ears. Robert was fast asleep again.

I had to stop for gas three more times on the journey. None of the other stations were as shoddy as the ones in Bumfuck, Nowhere (no, you literal dumbasses, that was not the real name of the town, however the place was such an insignificant blip on the radar of my life that I didn't bother to remember its real name), but they were close runners up. The first station had a shortage of gas, so they could only give out five gallons to each car. I was immediately reminded of the fuel rationing of the seventies. Thank god I wasn't alive for that, because I never would have driven again if that was the norm. The pumps at the second station didn't have a roof over them. This wouldn't have been a big deal, had it not been for the fact that the station seemed to have a never ending cloud of rain over top of it. I hadn't seen another cloud in the sky on the entire drive, but rain poured over me the entire time I filled the tank. The final station was a full-service station. I rang the bell by the pumps to signal the attendant. After twenty minutes of waiting, I'd grown so bored that I nearly got out of the car to pump the fuel myself, but the old man that ran the station hobbled out the door just as I was about to do so. I felt so bad for him that I didn't want to ruin his moment of glory. Wrong decision. It turns out that I would have been able to get out of the car and fill the tank myself and maybe do a few hundred laps around the parking lot in the amount of time it took him to reach my rental car. By the time he got to my car, several children had been conceived and birthed. Yet, somehow, the worst was still before me. It took the old man several minutes to locate the gas tank, despite the fact that it was in almost the same place on every vehicle. When he finally was able to locate it and insert the nozzle, he had to stop every few seconds to re-grip the handle. Whether that was because the pump didn't have a latch to hold itself in place or because the old man was too oblivious to know that such *advanced* technology existed, I didn't know. It took close to one hundred tries just to get one measly gallon of gas in the tank. I wanted to get out of the car and show the old man the correct way to do it, but I thought it best to save his pride. *See*, I'm much nicer than people give me credit for. That, and watching the old man struggle to fill up the tank was comedy unlike anything you could find on television. It was the highlight of my week. It almost made the whole trip worth it. Almost. I may have enjoyed comedy, but I was no fool.

When the gas station debacles were finally over, we were back on the road and on the home stretch. After just a few more miles of driving, I saw the sign for Cottonwood. As soon as we got within city limits, I pulled the car over. I wasn't going to waste one more second of my time in that shitbucket. I was tempted to abandon the sleeping Robert with the car, but I knew I couldn't. I knew I needed his help.

"Wakey wakey!" I yelled, violently shaking Robert. Startled, Robert defensively swung a fist at me, but I expertly avoided the blow.

He rubbed his eyes and looked out the window. "Finally there?"

For the first time in my life, I resisted making a sarcastic comment. "Yes we are. Welcome to *beautiful* Cottonwood, Georgia!" Well, I tried.

Chapter 21

Robert and I exited the vehicle and began to walk. I punched the address we'd found on the internet into Google Maps. It had been a bit of a risk to abandon the car. I didn't know how far away Alex Bellavick's house would be. It could have been miles for all I knew. Fortunately, I got my first stroke of luck of the day. The GPS said that it was only one-half mile to the house. I thought that to be an easy distance to walk. Not everyone agreed, however.

"My feet hurt. How much farther do we have to walk?" Robert bitched. I liked him better when he was asleep.

I turned around. "There's the car, Robert. We haven't even gone a block yet. I'm going to go out on a limb and say that we have a *little* bit more walking to do."

"I don't think I can make it. My feet are starting to get blistered." He picked up his right foot and showed me the blisters. I also caught a glimpse of the shoes he was wearing, though the term 'shoes' was a generous description. They looked more like sandals that had been fashioned out of old newspapers and a heavy amount of duct tape. I think I may have solved the mystery of why his feet were hurting.

"You mean those designer shoes aren't built for comfort and support?"

Robert immediately took offense to the comment. "Not all of us can afford fancy shoes like you. Some people spend every cent they can scrape together on silly things like food and water. Excuse me for not buying nice shoes. Next month, I'll go down to a thrift store and buy some shoes instead of eating."

"Do you see the shoes I'm wearing?" I held up my foot to show Robert. I thought he was going to be blinded by the shine. "These puppies cost me $2,000. They're made out of the finest leather money can buy. Guaranteed never to lose their shine. But my feet sweat horribly, if I wear them too long the balls of my feet bleed, and the odor has knocked me unconscious on more than one occasion. But those are the kinds of things you have to put up with if you want to be fashionable. Now, you don't hear me complaining about it, do you?"

Robert remained silent for the rest of the trek. It was a close second to him sleeping. We walked a few blocks, made a few turns, and then we were at Alex Bellavick's house.

The house was modest, but well taken care of. The lawn was neatly trimmed, the siding looked freshly painted, and the windows were so clean that it was necessary to close the shades at all times, lest they want passersby watching their every movement.

Robert and I walked to the door. I knocked as Robert stood by my side. A woman who we could only assume to be Bellavick's wife answered the door. She looked like she might have been pretty once, if not for the years of sleepless nights, hectic play dates, and mindless kid's shows numbing her brain.

"How can I help you?" she asked. She was friendly, like most people from a small town. Bad move on her part. I knew I could exploit that.

"Sorry to bother you, ma'am, but we'd like to speak with your husband." I turned on my legendary charm and flashed her a toothy grin.

"Are you friends of his?"

"Not exactly," I replied. "We just have a few questions to ask him."

"I don't understand. Is he in trouble for something?"

"No, no, no, nothing like that," I reassured her. I could tell she was skeptical. I had to think of something quick.

Luckily, that was not a foreign concept to me. "We're old friends of his from school. We just want to catch up with him and ask him about a few of our other old friends we've lost touch with. Is he home?"

"No, he's at work right now." Of course. How foolish of me to forget that not only did some people work a traditional job, some even worked *weekends*.

"Would you mind telling us where he works? We just have a few questions to ask him. We won't hold him up for too long," I said.

"I'm sorry, but I can't do that. You seem like...nice gentlemen, but my husband's never mentioned either of you before. If you want to come back in about an hour, he should be home then." She looked hesitantly at Robert as she spoke the word "nice". Not that I could blame her.

I was, however, glad that Robert had let me do all the talking. I was able to handle the situation much more smoothly than he would have been able to. Unfortunately, he picked the most inopportune time to pipe up.

"We're in a bit of a hurry," he began. "If you could just tell us where he works, that would be best for everyone." As he finished his sentence, Robert reached his hands down the front of pants. I cringed and Mrs. Bellavick panicked at the motion.

"He works down at the hardware store on the outskirts of town," she said, a look of terror in her eyes. "Please don't hurt him."

"We're not…" Robert began, but Mrs. Bellavick shut the door in his face and scurried away.

"We need to get out of here," I said, ushering Robert away from the house.

"Why? What did I do wrong? And why did she think that I was going to hurt him?" Robert was seemingly oblivious to his actions.

"Why the hell did you reach your hand down your pants?"

Robert blushed. He was embarrassed, but he answered. "These pants don't have any pockets, so I had put my journal in my waistband. I felt it slipping down, so I was just pulling it back up."

"Are you fucking kidding?" I was in disbelief. It was so stupid, but it had insinuated something so much more sinister. "Robert, it looked like you were grabbing for a gun. She's probably on the phone with the police as we speak. We need to get away in a hurry."

Robert and I briskly walked away. I got out my phone and searched for a hardware store in town. There was only one. Apparently Lady Luck was trying to make up for being a bitch earlier because the store was only a quarter of a mile away. If we hurried, we'd be able to get in and out of there before the police showed up.

We walked through the small residential section of town and came to a more rural area. There was a small abandoned shed, but no other buildings in sight. We passed through a small wooded area, using the trees for cover, and then saw the hardware store. It was small, but all that could be expected for a small town.

As we approached the store, I realized what an error we'd made. Neither of us had the slightest idea what Alex Bellavick looked like. How were supposed to be able to pick him from the lineup of workers at the hardware store?

When we crossed the threshold of the store, I realized my worry had been for naught. I'd only been in large hardware stores with many workers. The hardware store in Cottonwood only had two employees. One looked like he could have been the brother of the attendant from the final gas station. I felt safe assuming that he was not Mrs. Bellavick's husband. That meant it had to be the other guy.

The man we assumed to be Alex Bellavick was tall and handsome. Aside from looking the proper age, he also wore a wedding ring. Despite the fact that this was the only hardware store I'd ever been to where the employees didn't wear nametags, I was confident. This was our man.

Robert and I approached Alex Bellavick. In response to the small incident with Mrs. Bellavick, I convinced Robert to let me do all the talking, which he did not protest, though I sensed the decision did not sit well with him.

"Good afternoon," Alex Bellavick said, cheerfully. "How can I help you gentlemen today?

"Could we have a word with you?" I asked, trying to not to raise his alarm. It turns out that was unnecessary.

"Sure, I'd be more than happy to speak with you fellas." It was small town kindness at its finest. Bellavick was not the least bit suspicious. In fact, he was downright chipper, something that must have been difficult to maintain in a small town hardware store that likely saw very few customers.

"Would you mind if we went somewhere a bit more private?" I asked. "Maybe take a step outside?"

"I think that would be alright." He turned toward the old man, who looked half-asleep behind the counter. "Hey, Glenn, do you mind if I step outside for a minute and talk to these gentlemen?"

"Gee, I don't know. Do you think I can handle this rush all by myself?"

Bellavick chuckled and escorted us to the door. "That Glenn, always making wisecracks." He let out another loud chuckle, though neither Robert nor I shared in the amusement. Entertainment must not have been easy to come by in small towns.

We walked outside and stood in a circle on the edge of the hardware store's property line. There were no other buildings in the vicinity, no chance of being overheard. "So, what would the two of you like to discuss?" Bellavick asked.

"We wanted to talk about a few of your friends from school."

At the mention of old friends, Bellavick's eyes lit up. "Well, let's see, there's good old Jason. He was always a hoot. I still remember that time we stole his daddy's tractor. Ooee, I thought he was going to kill us after that. 'Specially after we drove into Mrs. Gladden's farm. I've never seen cows hightail it so quickly. And then you've got One-Eyed Charlie. Bet you can guess where he got the nickname. Lost his right eye to an unfortunately placed branch. Now he really has trouble seeing the forest for the trees. His real name's Darren. Not really sure where Charlie came from. And how could I forget Billy Sandstock? He spent all his time chasing after girls. In hindsight, maybe we should have seen the rape charge coming, but that's neither here nor there...I wonder what he's up to these days. And speaking of people I haven't seen in a while, Joe..."

"No you..." I bit my tongue at the word "idiot". I did not want to insult Alex Bellavick before he gave us the information we so desperately desired. That would have to wait until after our conversation. I'd already let his useless babbling go on for too long. We could not afford to waste

144

any more time. "I mean, we already had some people in mind that we wanted to ask you about." I reached inside my jacket pocket and pulled out the picture of the three men I'd printed. I pointed at the third, unknown man. "Could you tell us who this is?"

Bellavick grabbed the picture and studied it carefully. "It sure has been a long time since I was that age, but I don't seem to recognize any of these men."

In fairness, it had likely been more than forty years since the picture was taken, so I gave him the benefit of the doubt. Maybe he just needed a little help to jog his memory. I walked closer to Bellavick and identified the two men whose identities we did know. "This is Dale Showen. And the man standing next to him is Frank Davacchio."

Bellavick looked at the picture more closely, but seemed puzzled. "Dale Showen? And Frank Davaccio? You'll have to excuse me, but I don't believe I know anyone by either of those names."

He was playing stupid with us. There was something that he didn't want to tell us, and I was going to find out what that was, one way or another. "It really has been a long time. It's possible that those names may have slipped your mind. But I'm certain that you know them. You were the one who took this picture."

If it was possible, Bellavick looked at the picture even harder. He studied it from every angle, as if the different perspectives would help discern the subjects in some way. "I'm sorry, but I don't recognize any of these three men. I wish I could be more help." He seemed genuinely disappointed by his inability to provide assistance. He must have been prepared for our visit. Was it possible that Alex Bellavick was in on the plot as well? I would have suspected him to be the mastermind, but no one was that good at playing stupid.

We were running out of time and still had no answers. We needed to find a way to get him to talk. Robert, however, did not seem to feel the same sense of urgency. He walked away, unbeknownst to Bellavick. He picked up a sack of seed corn from the ground. What the hell was he doing? He emptied the sack on the ground. He was going to start playing with the corn. Was this really the time to look for entertainment? But then he did something that surprised both me and Alex Bellavick.

When the sack was empty, Robert darted over to Bellavick, placing it over the hardware store worker's head. Robert then restrained Bellavick's arms so that the man could not remove the bag. "Quick, grab his legs!" Robert urged.

"Robert?! What the hell are you doing?"

"We need to get him to talk and this is the only way I can think of. Now grab his legs before he squirms away!" Alex Bellavick had been too startled to react and process what was happening to him at first, but now he violently thrashed in Robert's arms, desperately trying to free himself. It was too late to back out now, so I grabbed Bellavick's legs and Robert and I began to walk.

"What now? We can't exactly take the bag off and say 'just kidding! This was all a big joke. Don't mind the sack on your head. We're just having a little fun!'"

"I know that, Julian. I'm not a moron. There's an abandoned shed through the trees. We can bring him there while we figure out how to get him to talk." He was right. Wow, that was a weird thought. Robert actually right about something? Talk about signs of the apocalypse.

Robert and I carried the man to the shed. I was in good shape, but it still wasn't easy to carry a full grown man, especially one that was constantly writhing to be freed. Sweat covered my body by the time we got him to the shed. And the suit I wore was not designed to handle such a strenuous workout. I was starting to think there might be a niche market for a more activewear line of suits.

When we got to the shed, Robert and I set Bellavick in an old wooden chair. I did my best to restrain the man while Robert searched for a rope. He returned shortly thereafter with an old, frayed rope, about ten feet in length. It wouldn't hold Bellavick forever, but it would do the job. That is, if we were able to get him to start talking in a reasonable amount of time.

As soon as the rope was fastened around Bellavick's arms and legs to Robert's satisfaction, I turned to him. "Now what? What's your grand plan to get him to talk?"

"I'll get him to talk. You just leave this to me."

I was glad to let Robert take the lead on this one. I'd already tried and failed. I was out of ideas. I might as well see what he could do.

Robert pulled the sack from Bellavick's head. "Now that you see that we're not fucking around, why don't you tell us what we want to know? Who is the third man? Don't bother playing stupid anymore. It won't do you any good. And don't even think about trying to yell for help. No one will be able to hear you from here." I don't know how Robert could have possibly known that. There was no way. He was bluffing, but I wasn't going to open my mouth and spoil that.

"I'm telling the truth. I don't know any of those people. Please. You have to believe me." Alex Bellavick looked terrified. He tried to wiggle free, but when he was unable to do so, his panic only grew worse. "I have a family. A wife and kids. Please, don't hurt me."

"Maybe you should think about cooperating then. How about a little refresher. That oughta get the memories flowing again." Robert held the picture in front of Bellavick's face to give him another look.

Alex Bellavick again examined the photo, trying his hardest to identify anyone in the picture, hoping that he may be able to recall something. When Robert pulled the picture away, I saw a tear run down Bellavick's cheek. "Please, I don't know anything. Please believe me!"

Robert wasn't buying it. "So, it seems that they've convinced you not to talk. No matter. I'll get you to talk. You can be sure of that." Say what you will about the guy, he could be a hardass when he wanted to. I sure would not have wanted to be on the receiving end of his interrogation, but I would never let him know that.

Robert walked away from the restrained man and motioned for me to join him. "It's not going to be easy to get him to talk. We're going to have to do some things, some unpleasant things. But we need to get him to talk."

"What do you mean?"

Robert lowered his voice so that Bellavick could not hear the conversation. "You're a smart man, Julian." He spoke without sarcasm or condescension. "We'll never get to the bottom of this by playing nice. We need to get him to talk by any means necessary. We need to resort to something more drastic."

Robert and I both knew what he was referring to, though neither of us said it. Torture.

I gulped nervously, but fortunately, Robert did not notice. I was willing to do just about anything to find out who was behind all of this, but torture? That was a different kind of animal. I'd told myself a long time ago that violence was not the means to an end. I'd learned that lesson the hard way sixteen years ago. "Robert, are you sure that's the best way? That's the only way to get him to talk?"

"Do you have a better solution?"

He didn't even bother to wait for my answer (though I had none). And deep down, I knew he was right. Robert was right (twice in one day? I must have been going mad). Was it just me or was he starting to make more sense? He sounded less neurotic and he was laser-focused on getting the information we needed. He was beginning to sound - dare I say- *logical*. And he hadn't complained in, like, ten minutes. That was the most telling sign of all.

Robert surveyed the area, looking for anything to serve as a makeshift torture device. Though the shed had yielded a chair and rope in our time of need, it certainly was no punisher's chamber. The choices were scarce, and it came as no surprise to me when he returned empty handed.

"Figures there'd be nothing useful here," he said. "That would have been too convenient."

Ah, back to normal. "So what do we do now?" I asked.

"I suppose we could just try hitting him."

I held my hands out in front of me. "These things are far too pretty to be hitting anyone. Besides, punching people seems like it hurts. I'm not trying to torture myself."

"You're right." He thought to himself for a moment. "I have an idea."

Robert approached Alex Bellavick and removed the sack from his head. Then he proceeded with what I can only describe as an updated method of "Bam slapping". He opened both of his hands and slapped the man across the face quickly and repeatedly. The blows weren't powerful, but they were just strong enough to be annoying. Maybe he was going for the same type of effect as the Chinese water torture. His *brilliant* idea didn't work, however. Bellavick only seemed to be about as bothered as someone fending off a pesky mosquito, nowhere near enough to reveal the information he'd been withholding.

Nothing to worry about, though; Robert was not going to give up that easily. Robert cocked his foot to give Bellavick a swift kick to the shin. It was a much better idea than slapping and probably would have worked, had Bellavick not jostled the chair at the last second, causing Robert to kick the leg of the chair instead. Robert howled in pain and hopped on his left foot, trying to massage the pain out of his right. Once he was able to stand on both feet again, he attempted a kick with his left foot, so as to not worsen his injury. Unfortunately, however, Robert was not ambipedal. He missed Bellavick and the chair all together, and the force of the swing landed him on his back with a hard thud. If Robert had not replaced the bag on our captive's head, Bellavick surely would have been laughing hysterically at the feeble attempts. It even took great willpower for me not to burst out laughing.

Over the course of the next ten minutes, Robert tried various other methods of torture, while I tried to aid as best as I could. He first brought up waterboarding, though he did not know the proper method of execution. I told him everything I knew: that it involved pouring water on the victim. It wasn't much to go off of, but it was more than Robert offered, so he improvised. Robert left the sack on Bellavick's head, and poured about a gallon of water over the prisoner's head from a Culligan jug that was in the corner of the shed. It did not have the desired effect, so he continued to pour two more gallons. Still nothing, so Robert emptied the jug. Yet, it still produced no results. I still had no idea how that was supposed to earn any sort of confession.

Robert's next great idea: tickling. Don't laugh; it had really been used before. Robert's theory was that excessive tickling could cause such unbearable agony and hysteria that Bellavick would not be able to endure it. Robert tried everything. He tickled the man's armpits, his feet, his sides, but the best he was able to produce was the laugh of a giddy schoolgirl.

When he gave up on that, Robert tried "defecation interrogation". There were several large piles of animal manure outside the shed. For this method of torture, Robert removed the sack from Bellavick's head. He grabbed handfuls of poop and lobbed them at the man. Several splattered against his face, but still the man retained that he knew nothing. So, Robert decided that a more aggressive approach was necessary. Rather than continuing to throw the feces, Robert smeared handfuls all over the man's face. The odor must have been horrific. He repeated this until he was finally able to get some of the poop in the man's mouth. This got Bellavick to open his mouth, but it was not the result that Robert desired. Instead of telling us the identity of the third man, Bellavick proceeded to vomit all over Robert. A great blast spewed on Robert's face, and in a stroke of karma, some even landed in his mouth. That was enough to get Robert to move on.

After Robert cleaned himself (and I had a laugh at his expense), he walked toward me to regroup. "We're out of options. We need to cause pain. It's the only way." He sounded dejected as he spoke, but his eyes told a different story. They looked almost...excited about the idea. That horrified me.

His words and body language disheartened me, but I knew he was right. That was third time that day. I told myself that I would schedule a mental health evaluation when we got back to the city. "Alright," I said. I was barely able to get the word out of my mouth.

Robert found a crowbar hidden under an old tarp. He swung the instrument twice - once at each leg. It was an unmistakable noise, the ear-splitting sound of shattering bone. "Please - I don't know anything - I swear I don't know anything - you must believe me," Bellavick pleaded. He spoke through sobs. But Robert was not ready to give up so easily.

He sent a blow to each of the man's arms and another to his ribs. Bellavick whimpered in pain. "Just tell us what we want to know and this is all going to stop." The voice that spoke was Robert's but it didn't sound like him. He sounded cold and maniacal, almost evil.

Bellavick did not respond. So, Robert continued. He hit Bellavick's body, his legs, his arms, then, finally, a few shots to his head. He was careful not to do too much damage. He did not want to kill the man or cause him to lose consciousness. Robert seemed to get some wicked sort of satisfaction out of the brutal beating. At that moment, I realized there was a Robert that I didn't know. A sick, twisted, deranged lunatic who seemed to get pleasure out of inflicting pain upon others.

Then something happened, something that I cannot I explain. As Robert continued to beat the man, a splitting headache erupted in the back of my head. It was pain like I'd never felt before. It was overwhelming and I dropped to my knees. Suddenly, visions passed through my mind, glimpses of the past. I was holding a gun. Then I heard a gunshot. Then I was standing over a bleeding man. The worst moment of my life. Something I could never take back. The visions raced through my mind, tormenting me, tearing at every fiber of my being.

I summoned the strength to open my eyes, to break away from the scenes. Robert's barrage had caused Bellavick's wallet to fall on the ground. I don't know what compelled me, but I picked it up. Maybe I thought it would be the key to our answer. I looked through it, but it was empty, except for a couple credit cards and a ten dollar bill. Then I looked at the ID and I was overcome with dread. It felt like my insides had been violently torn from my body.

Robert didn't say a word as I blankly stared into the corner. I don't even know if he noticed. When I was able to formulate words again, I turned to him and threw the wallet. "It's not him. We got the wrong guy."

Chapter 22

Robert and I didn't say a word as we left the shed. We heard sirens coming our direction, but we were safely under the cover of trees. Only when the sound faded did we feel comfortable venturing back onto the main street. Though it was a small town, they did have one car rental agency. We high-tailed it there and got a car without a problem. Say what you will about podunk towns, but at least their businesses don't jerk you around. They actually stock the goods they claim to sell.

I was still in shock from the mistaken identity. I triple checked that we'd had the right address (we did). Alex Bellavick must have moved recently, but the directories hadn't been updated to reflect that. There was nothing we could do. At least that's what I told myself.

I couldn't tell where Robert's head was at. His facial expression remained indifferent; it revealed nothing. I could not tell if he felt remorse or apathy. For my own sanity, I chose to believe that, though he didn't show it, the former was true, even though I wasn't sure he was truly capable of showing remorse.

Though we knew we needed to get out of the town quickly, we could not leave empty handed. We chanced a stop at the sole gas station in town to inquire about Alex Bellavick. It was a small enough town that everybody knew each other. If Alex Bellavick moved, there was a chance that the attendant would know where.

When we got to the gas station, Robert offered to go in to ask about Bellavick. It was not like him to do something just out of the kindness of his heart. Maybe he wanted to feel like he actually contributed something. Or maybe he trying make up for violently abusing the innocent man. Whatever his reason, I didn't question him. I was still too shaken from the torture to want to talk to anyone. So, despite the fact that I knew I would have a better chance at success at my absolute worst than Robert and his homely appearance at his absolute best, I let him walk in.

After more than ten minutes, Robert still had not returned. What the hell was he doing in there? Did he stop at the bathroom to work one out quick? Did he get mesmerized by all the food options inside? Surely that looked like a smorgasbord to him. It was nice to feel my sense of humor returning. I was starting to feel like myself again. But then a dark thought crossed my mind. What if he'd been caught inside? Would they come outside looking for an accomplice? Would Robert turn me in in hopes of saving himself?

As is the case of most things that worry you, my worries about Robert came to pass. He walked out of the gas station about five minutes later, and judging from the ear-to-ear grin on his face, he'd succeeded in finding the whereabouts of the real Alex Bellavick. He entered the rental car with such a smug look on his face that I wanted to continue our silence, but I thought better of it. I knew I needed his information.

"You better not have come back empty-handed after spending all that time dicking around in there," I said. I wasn't going to give him too much satisfaction. He was still an ungrateful prick.

"You bet your ass I found out where Alex Bellavick is living. You really shouldn't doubt me, Julian," he replied. "You're not the only one who can be a smooth talker. You should have seen me in there. The guy behind the counter was a real asshole. He didn't want to give up any information, but I turned my charm on and eventually he told me. I was everything you think you are, a regular panty dropper." Robert, a smooth talker? The idea was more than laughable. I'd only guessed that humility was not one of his virtues. Oh how I underestimated that. I could hardly fathom the steaming pile of bullshit he would spew if I'd been foolish enough to offer him praise. Fortunately, I wasn't that stupid.

"Well..." I said, trying to get the information out of him. After all, that was the reason we'd come all this way. Robert must have lost track of that while he gloated and looked longingly at me for praise.

"Well what?" he asked. I could not tell if he was playing a fool or if it was because he really *was* a fool.

Still, I had to indulge him. But only a little bit. "Where does Bellavick live? You did go through *all* the trouble of finding that information."

His eyes lit up in the blissful ignorance of my sarcasm. "I thought you'd never ask!" he jovially exclaimed. "Here's his address." Robert handed me a crumpled up napkin to examine, which was oddly fitting for him.

"Good," I said. "He doesn't live too far from here. It should only be a twenty minute drive or so."

"Yeah, I guess he moved away to open up a restaurant. He should probably be there now. The name of his place should be on there." Robert looked at me, as if expecting more praise. Jesus Christ, you'd think he'd cured cancer or solved world hunger. How did he have the audacity to call me the arrogant one? Sure, I wasn't going to admit to being the most humble person, but he was every bit as bad as I was. He just had less to be proud of.

We got out of the town without incident and began the journey to the real Alex Bellavick's restaurant, The Caribbean Crusade. I'd bet my life's savings that a Caribbean restaurant would not be successful business venture in rural Florida, but I doubted anyone would be stupid enough to take that bet. I wondered what could possibly have compelled him to open it. If, like many owners of small restaurants, he was following his life's dream, then his life's dream must have been to fail magnificently and piss away his money.

Robert remained quiet for the trip and I did not make any attempt to make conversation. I knew why I was silent - I couldn't bear to listen to another second of him bragging about how he'd been able to get the information for us. The second time around, the story probably would have to devolved to something along the lines of him fighting off a band of ninjas, saving a beautiful princess and being rewarded with a quickie, then using hypnosis to put the clerk in such a deep trance that he was forced to reveal the information. It made me sick just thinking about it. As far as the reason Robert kept quiet, I could only speculate, but it seemed more than likely that he was sulking because I hadn't given him the praise he thought he deserved. If I could continue to think of ways to offend him, maybe I'd never have to talk to him again. If only I could be so lucky.

Twenty minutes later, Robert and I arrived in Delta, Florida. It was smaller even than Cottonwood - the kind of town that bred racism and still denied that the Civil Rights Act had been officially passed by Congress. It was the kind of place that would have happily subscribed to a rebirth of slavery. I couldn't wait to see how Robert fit in there.

It was not difficult to find The Caribbean Crusade. It was located right on the main drag, between a church and a bar. Aside from the gas station across the street, it did not appear that there were any other businesses in the small town. On our way to the restaurant, we saw more tractors than cars, and the only thing that outnumbered the amount of people in overalls in the town was the number of teeth that its residents were missing.

The restaurant was small, but from the outside it appeared that most of the tables were empty. Located just beneath the sign that bore the eatery's name was a banner that read, *The Only Jerk You'll Be Needing Tonight*. I could tell this was going to be fun.

We walked inside and waited to be seated. We decided it best to eat a meal before summoning Alex Bellavick. The reasons for doing so were twofold: we hadn't eaten all day and Bellavick would likely be more trusting of paying customers.

For a place that was almost completely empty, it took much longer for us to get a seat than it should have. The waitstaff was not exactly on their toes.

Robert and I sat at our table and waited for a waitress to take our order. While we waited, I surveyed the restaurant, hoping to see Alex Bellavick. I watched every person in the restaurant, but none of them seemed to be our man, nor did any of them appear to be the owner.

"I don't think he's here," I told Robert, dejectedly.

"How would you know? You have no idea what he looks like."

"I know he's a he, so that rules out about three quarters of the people here. And everyone else is either too old or too young or too not-white."

Robert didn't like that. "How do you know he's white? You don't think a minority would be able to open up a restaurant? You probably think all black people are poor like me."

I may not have had many black friends, but that didn't mean I was racist against them, as Robert insinuated. Now poor people, that was a different story, but I had no problem with black people. So long as they weren't poor.

"I know intelligence isn't exactly your forte, but think about it for a minute. Dale Showen and Frank Davacchio are rich, white men. They probably grew up going to fancy prep schools in the sixties that would have laughed at any minority applicants. And Davacchio is a member of the Tea Party, the most conservative faction of the Republican party. There's no way they would have been caught dead associating with a minority. That was probably the way that their parents raised them. Alex Bellavick is definitely white."

Robert looked at me defiantly, desperately trying to refute my point, but he gave up. He was defeated. "What are we supposed to do now?"

"I'm not sure. We can eat our food and hope Bellavick shows up by the time we're done with our meal. If not, maybe one of the employees can tell us where he is or where he lives."

Robert did not seem impressed by the suggestion. He surveyed the restaurant himself probably hoping that he could be the hero again. He stared for a suspiciously long time at the kitchen. Then his eyes lit up. "I have an idea," he said.

I was hoping he would just offer the information himself, but Robert did not continue. I should have known better than to think anything else. "Let's hear this *great* idea," I said. Trying to get information out of him was worse than pulling fucking teeth (though Robert seemed to be getting a kick out of it).

"Everyone back in the kitchen is black. I doubt they'd notice if one more person joined them." Apparently Robert's casual racism was acceptable, but my assumption and underlying logic identifying Bellavick as white was offensive. "So, I'm going to sneak back there and pretend like I'm a worker to get the inside scoop on Alex Bellavick. You know, since I'm so good at this reconnaissance thing."

And there he goes: right back to bragging about the clerk. It wasn't like he'd convinced a hot nun to have sex with him. That, I would have applauded him for. "I just don't see the point. We can just ask our waitress if we don't end up seeing Bellavick."

"You saw how freaked out that lady got in Cottonwood when we started asking questions. People don't want to give up that kind of information so easily."

He had a point. And this was now the fourth time I'd agreed with Robert. One more time, and I'd find a nice high bridge to drive off of on our way back to the city. Still, Robert's plan was full of holes. This was a small restaurant. All the employees had to know each other. And if they didn't, was Robert believable as an employee? Nothing about his appearance suggested that he should be cooking food for anyone. We needed a better plan.

As Robert continued to persuade me of the validity of his plan (which had about as much chance of success as Tuvalu winning a war against America - if you've never heard of Tuvalu, that's the point, that's how fucking stupid Robert's idea was), I saw the waitress looking at me out of the corner of my eye. I tried to return her look, but she turned away in embarrassment. That was the third time I'd seen her looking at me, and it didn't take a PhD to know that she was smitten.

"You know what, Robert," I said after she looked over a fourth time, "why don't you give it a shot? I'll...I'll...uh...be looking for clues elsewhere."

Robert jumped at the opportunity to test out his plan. He tried to walk to the kitchen nonchalantly, but I'd never seen someone who looked more chalant. As much as he tried to play coy, he drew quite a few looks. Fortunately, none were from the staff. He crossed the threshold of the kitchen and immediately found an apron. He put it on, but after that he disappeared. I couldn't tell how things were going, but the fact that he wasn't kicked out at first sight boded well for him.

"What can I get you to drink?" I hadn't noticed anyone approaching. I was too busy trying to catch a glimpse of Robert. When I finally processed what had happened and looked at the waitress, I couldn't believe I didn't notice. She was even more stunning up close. I honestly couldn't believe I hadn't been staring at her from the moment we walked in the door. She had curly blonde hair, electric green eyes, a face that was far too pretty for a town this hickish, and a curvaceous body. I wanted to play the bongos on her ass and squeeze her tits like a stress ball.

"Just a water will be fine," I said when I was finally able to shake myself out of her trance.

"I'll have that up for you in just a second." My eyes were glued to her ass from the second she walked away. And when she walked past, I had to pretend to be looking at something just past her so that it wasn't too obvious that I was staring at her breasts.

"What happened to your friend?" she asked when she returned with my water.

"He..." I started, but did not have a chance to finish the lie before she interrupted. That was my biggest pet peeve. What was the fucking point of asking a question if you're just going to answer it yourself? This might not seem like the most appropriate time to be complaining about this, but that had always irked me. If she hadn't been hot enough that I was still fighting to get rid of my boner, I might have said something to her. But she was so hot.

"Did he leave because of the reports of E. coli here? Because those are lies. Most of them at least."

"No he..."

"Was it because he heard the cooks cum in people's food? Because that was just one cook and it only happened one time. And to be fair, that guy did sleep with his girlfriend?"

"Actually, I think he just stepped outside for a moment," I quickly answered, mortified to hear any more of her speculative reasons for Robert's departure.

I flashed her a toothy grin, though it was as much for my own benefit. She responded by blushing. I knew she was mine. I nodded my head to the bathroom, and the waitress turned around on the spot. For a second, I thought she'd refused my advances, but then she motioned for me to follow. That was, without a doubt, the least work I'd done to get laid. I guess it isn't often these small town girls get a chance at a man like me.

About twenty minutes later, I returned from the bathroom. It would have been a shock if none of the other patrons had heard the waitress's loud moaning, but I couldn't have given a fuck less. Was it my fault that I knew how to satisfy a lady?

I sat back down to an empty table. What the hell was Robert doing? How was he not back yet? I knew his plan was delusional. Surely he'd been caught in the act. Unfortunately, I did not have time to dwell on the situation for too long. The waitress walked over and started to talk to me. Why were they always so clingy? That was why I always kicked them out after sex. I couldn't bear to suffer through childhood stories and feelings and shit like that. The waitress began to spend an inordinate amount of time at my table, making any excuse to return, filling up my glass of water after only a few sips, and repeatedly asking if I'd decided what I wanted to eat, despite the fact that I hadn't opened my menu.

Finally, after about twenty more minutes, Robert emerged from the kitchen. He threw his apron over his head and darted for the table, looking panicked.

"What's wrong?" I asked. "And what took you so long?"

"Well, I got back to the kitchen and there was no one else back there. I don't know where all the cooks went. I poked around a little, but I couldn't find anyone or any useful information. Right as I was about to leave, one of the waiters came back and said he was waiting for four orders and gave me two more to cook up. I didn't want to blow our cover, so I gave it my best shot. I was never a good cook before I was homeless and it's been more than ten years since I've actually cooked anything." I looked around and saw several patrons trying their best to choke down their food. Another made a beeline for the bathroom, a hand covering his mouth. "Anyway, I had to stay back there until I finished cooking everything."

"That's not so bad. So you cooked up some shitty food. What's the problem with that?"

"There's more to the story." I was terrified to find out what that meant. "I'm not exactly sure how it happened, but after I finished the last meal, there was a bit of an incident. A small fire may have started." Robert must have seen the look in my eyes because he immediately tried to convince me that it wasn't a big deal. "I'm sure they have procedures in place for an event such as that. It'll be just fine. I'm sure of it."

Chapter 23

The sirens that raced down the street clearly said the situation was anything but fine. The whole restaurant had been evacuated as the building was slowly engulfed in flames. By the time the fire department arrived, the fire was roaring. The good news, however, was that there was no way Bellavick wouldn't show up now.

A man, presumably Alex Bellavick, exited a vehicle a few minutes later. Upon the site, he dropped to his knees, pleading. "My restaurant! My restaurant!"

He talked to the firefighters and his employees, desperately trying to determine a cause for the disaster. One of the waiters spoke animatedly, then pointed at Robert. So much for keeping a low profile. There was no way we were going to get away with this. Robert's face incriminated him. Bellavick marched to us.

"What the hell are you two doing here?" Bellavick asked. His tone was calm, but he couldn't hide the bitterness in his voice. Who could blame him after what Robert did?

"We wanted to talk to you actually."

"And just *asking* me to talk was too difficult?" Bellavick sharply retorted.

"Right," I jumped in. "It's 2016. No one just goes up and talks to people these days. You have to talk on the Internet for at least a week or two first."

"I think there's a lesson to be learned here," Bellavick snidely replied. "How about next time you want to talk someone, do it the old fashioned way, instead of burning down their fucking restaurant." I surveyed the scene of our destruction and realized that Alex Bellavick had a point. But our way was more fun.

"Look," Robert began, "the bottom line is that we want to talk to you. You are Alex Bellavick, right?"

"And if I'm not, does that mean that I went through all of this for nothing?" Bellavick shot back.

I knew from the interaction that this was our man. He had a certain curiosity about him, like he knew our presence wasn't without cause. Still, you could never be too sure. We'd learned that lesson already. "It could be worse," I said without elaborating. "I'll pay for the damages. We just need to know if you really are Alex Bellavick."

"You're damn right you're going to pay for the damages," the man highly suspected of being Alex Bellavick said in a condescending tone. "But, yes, I am Alex Bellavick."

"Thank God," I said, probably a little too relieved, but I could not stand harming another innocent person. Robert may have been indifferent on the matter, had it not been for a burning desire (no pun intended) to find answers.

"Let's get to what you wanted to talk about before you cause any more damage."

I didn't comment on the fact that there was little else we could do to further damage the building. I grabbed the picture from jacket pocket and handed it to Bellavick. "Do you recognize these men?"

Bellavick furrowed his eyebrows as he studied the photo for a few seconds, but then his eyes opened wide in a horrific realization. "I can't help you."

"You do recognize them." I knew he did. I saw it in his eyes. He knew the men and there was something that he didn't want to tell us.

"It doesn't matter. I can't help you. Get out of here and don't come back." Bellavick seemed skittish as he spoke. The once confident, powerful man was consumed by cowardice and insecurity.

Robert started to walk away. I couldn't believe he was going to give up that easily. It was probably just a reflex for him. Surely, being asked to leave the premises of a restaurant could not be a foreign concept to Robert. I, on the other hand, stood my ground.

"Can't help us? Or won't help us?" I asked. I looked Bellavick up and down with an expressionless face.

Bellavick wandered closer to the remnants of his restaurant. He picked a broken shard of a glass off the ground and wiped it down with his shirt. He was either doing this because of the nerves or he was preparing to stab me. I was really hoping for the former.

Finally, he set the piece of glass down and said, "Won't. I won't help you."

Robert must have realized that I wasn't going anywhere anytime soon because he walked back over. I shook my head in disbelief at Bellavick, then scoffed. "I should have known that you were a coward from the moment I met you. That's why you moved out here, isn't it? They found out where you lived and you were too much of a chicken-shit pussy to stand your ground. So, you ran off to some small little hick town and hoped they wouldn't come sniffing around for you again."

Bellavick balled his right hand into a fist. For a second, I thought he was going to punch me. That was what I wanted. I wanted him to get angry and start spewing off the information that he was so desperate to keep concealed. But then his look changed. The fire in his eyes died. He nervously gulped. "You have no idea who you're dealing. You have no idea what they're capable of."

"Actually, we know exactly what they're capable of. They killed a...a friend of mine." I normally wouldn't have described Trevor as a "friend", but I figured that was going to help me more than calling him 'this junky hacker guy I know'.

"Then you know exactly why I can't help you," Bellavick said. "I have a family. I can't put them at risk. If it was just me, that would be one thing, but I can't put them in harm's way. Besides, those guys - the ones in the picture - haven't done anything to me. I have no reason to turn on them."

"They might not have harmed you or anyone in your family, but what about the people they have harmed? The ones that didn't have anyone to defend them or to fight back for them and avenge them? Don't they mean anything? These are evil, callous men who will stop at nothing to get what they want. They don't care who gets in their way. They will crush them like a bug and dispose of them in the same way. I've had enough of that. I'm going to be the one that takes them down and finally puts an end to all of this, with or without your help. It might make things a little harder, it might take a little longer, but I won't stop until those three men are lying in their graves and I'm standing over them, beer in hand." I don't know where all the passion came from. I'd just started talking and the words just came to me. I'd never been more determined to stop those men than in that moment. If that hadn't convinced Bellavick to help, then nothing would.

Bellavick stood silently, thinking about what I'd said. And then he continued to just stand there. And then he stood some more, still in silence. I actually thought he might have fallen asleep with his eyes open, but then he blinked a few times. It was like watching Ben Carson in the debates. The silence persisted so long that I honestly didn't care what his decision was, so long as he made one this millennium. Finally, Bellavick said, "It's not going to be easy." He did not acknowledge the long silence, nor did he seem to think it out of the ordinary.

"So, does that mean you're going to help us?" I asked him, quickly waking from my daydream, which had gone on for so long that I was fighting a gigantic and surprisingly muscular teddy bear that Robert morphed into.

"I don't think I could have been more clear," he said.

"Actually, I think you could have. Just a simple 'yes' or 'no' would have been helpful. Your answer seemed to imply that you intend to help us, but you could have easily issued the same statement without agreeing to help. And such a long period of indecision only further muddies the waters of your previous statement, so a little more clarity would be appreciated."

I wasn't sure how Bellavick would react to my condescending tone. In retrospect, it probably wasn't the smartest thing to do; we had just destroyed his restaurant after all. But he remained even keeled. "I can tell you what I know, but that's all the help I'm willing to provide."

"That's all we can ask for. We couldn't ask you to put you or your family at risk," I lied, convincingly. He was just another pawn in my plan to figure out who the mastermind was, and I'd discovered that pawns respond better after being flattered.

"I appreciate that. I'd also appreciate if you you didn't mention my name if you get caught." Both Robert and I nodded in agreement, so Bellavick continued. "Their names are Frank Davacchio, Dale Showen, and Carson Gorelli."

"Caron Gorelli! He's the one we're looking for."

"He lives in the city, somewhere up in Groveland Heights. I don't know exactly where."

"Do you know where he works, or what he looks like now, or anything else that might be helpful?"

"I don't. That's everything I know. I realize it isn't a whole lot, but it should at least get you started in the right direction. Carson Gorelli is a very secretive man. It won't be easy to find out any information about him."

Good, I thought. Just what we needed, another wild goose chase. I was starting to think that Robert was right about being on a never ending trail of breadcrumbs. But I would never admit that to him. As promised, I was already searching for mental institutions and bridges near me on my phone.

Robert and I started to leave, but Alex Bellavick stopped us before we got to the curb. "Aren't you guys forgetting something?"

"You're right," I said. I pulled out my wallet and handed him ten dollars. "That oughta cover our drinks."

"You know what? Your drinks are on the house. Anything else?"

"Not that I can think of." I paused for a brief second. "Are you one of those d-bags that makes people say thank you for everything?"

"No. It's not that."

"Good," I replied, and we turned around to leave again. But once again, Bellavick stopped us.

"Nothing else. You're not forgetting anything else?" Bellavick must have noticed our blank stares because he decided to stop being so fucking cryptic. "God damn it. I thought you said you were going to pay for all the damage."

"Oh, right," I said. I reached into my pocket and signed a check, which I handed to Bellavick. "I know this is more outdated than cash, but it's the best I've got."

Robert and I turned to leave for the third time, and this time we left unimpeded. We walked back to the car and made our way back to the city.

Chapter 24

After I dropped Robert off, I returned the rental car to one of the affiliates in town and walked back to my apartment. Despite what Bellavick said, I decided to try to do some digging on Carson Gorelli. This time, however, I chose to do my research from the comfort of my own home. As *excited* as I was to see the librarian again, without Robert, it was unnecessary for me to return. *Shoot.*

If Gorelli really lived in Groveland Heights like Bellavick suggested, he was not going to be easy to track down. Groveland Heights was arguably the most exclusive community, not just in Florida, but in the entire country. It boasted more billionaires than the rest of the country combined. How such a mecca for the uber-wealthy arose in northern Florida, no one really knew. The community was surrounded by more guards and grandiose gated fences than the country club I belonged to. It was my ultimate goal to live there one day. However, despite my considerable wealth, I would have been the poorest person to live there by far, and that sure as hell wasn't going to fly with me.

After a few minutes of research, it quickly became evident that Bellavick was right about Carson Gorelli's privacy. I couldn't find a single article, biography, or passage about him. I couldn't even find a fucking Facebook page - unless he was a sexually confused fourteen year old boy in Alabama (sidebar: how shitty must life be for that kid? That's like being a straight person in San Francisco). It was not going to be easy to track him down. I went to bed defeated, vowing to try again the next day.

The next morning, I woke up to my phone ringing. That was twice now that someone called me, which meant it was time to get a new phone.

"What the hell do you want?" I asked, picking up the phone.

"Well that's no way to answer your phone," a jolly voice on the other end replied. It sounded familiar, but I couldn't place it. I did, however, know that it wasn't the person I suspected. That only made me angrier. I might as well just post the number on a billboard at this point.

"Oh was that not cordial enough?" I started, sarcastically. "My apologies. Let me start again. Who the fuck are you and how the fuck did you get this number?"

"I can't say that's a lot better, but you did inquire about my identity, so it's a step in the right direction."

"Will you just tell me what the hell this is about, so we can both get on with our lives?"

"There's another step: the swear words are getting less aggressive. Anyway, I'm calling because we never got your rental car back yesterday."

"How did you get this number?" I asked. "It wasn't easy. The number you gave us wasn't in service anymore. We tried searching for you in the book, but all we found was what sounded like an old, gay, black man. Then my manager had the great idea to try the caller ID. But, of course, that button is broken on our phone. So is the speaker button. And the number 3. Well, that gave me the idea to try the old *69 trick, and here we are."

Leave it to Trevor to be bested in such a simple way. He was always so focused on high-tech, detailed security that he let the little things slip by. "Sounds like you went through quite the...wait a minute. I called you almost twenty-four hours ago. You mean to tell me that you haven't gotten any calls since then?"

"For some reason, we really don't get too many calls." I wonder why that is.

"Weird. But I honestly didn't think you guys would miss that car."

"The auditor did describe that vehicle as 'not only the first asset that had to be classified as a liability, but a serious risk for explosion, probable carbon monoxide hazard, and a small possibility of being an earthquake catalyst.' Maybe we would be better off without it."

"So, I really did you a favor?"

"I guess so."

"Are we done here?"

"Yes, sir. You have a peachy day."

"It's off to such a great start, I don't know how it could possibly get any better." I hung up the phone before the clerk could respond.

Now that I was done wasting my time with meaningless phone calls from blissfully idiotic rental car clerks, it was time to focus on the tasks at hand. Most importantly, I needed to track down the whereabouts of Carson Gorelli. That had already proven to be a difficult task, and I didn't foresee it getting any easier. And if I was somehow able to do that, then I needed to get Robert cleaned up for our potential future meeting. While I was perfectly willing to let him go into some little hick town in his current appearance, he would stick out like a disfigured and heavily bandaged sore thumb in Groveland Heights. The mere sight of him would have warranted at least a half dozen calls to the police.

Ever wonder where the phrase "I look like a homeless person" originated? Look no further than Robert. And as much as I wanted to talk to Carson Gorelli myself, something in my gut told me that Robert would have a role to play.

Since I'd hit a brick wall in tracking Gorelli, I decided to focus on the second task. Before parting ways, Robert and I planned to meet to discuss the next stop in our traveling circus of ass clownery.

Prior to arriving at his motel, I called around to several local barbershops and full-service salons to try to schedule Robert an appointment. It was not easy to find a place with an opening, especially after I warned them about Robert. Eventually, though, I did find one daring soul at an obscure full-service salon that was willing to take on the challenge.

A few hours later, I set out to meet Robert. Like usual, he was nowhere to be found when I arrived. Seriously, would it fucking kill him to be on time just once? After five minutes, my patience ran thin. I stormed through the motel lobby to Robert's room. I about kicked through the door before I remembered that I had a key to the room in my wallet. Out of politeness, I knocked on Robert's bedroom door. My patience had worn so low that I waited less than ten seconds before opening the door. Sure as shit, there Robert was, fast asleep in bed. I wanted to wring his neck. But I was going to have a little bit of fun with him.

182

First, I poked his cheek. He didn't even budge. I knew he was a heavy sleeper, but I didn't expect him to rival a bear in hibernation. Then, I poked his face much harder. Still, not even as much as a stir. Heavy sleeper didn't even begin to describe it. There was, of course, a chance he was dead. But I was willing to take my chances. Back in my younger days, I would have covered him head to foot in sharpie tattoos of penises and other juvenile images. But I was more mature than that. Still, I couldn't resist a little juvenile humor, so I drew a small sign that read *Insert Here* on the small of his back with an arrow pointing to his asshole.

Not wanting to waste any more time, I decided to definitively wake Robert up. I tilted the mattress until he slid off it and crashed to the ground.

"Ugh, what happened?" Robert asked, rubbing his head. "Was there an earthquake?"

I hoped Robert didn't notice me because that was one of the dumbest things I'd ever heard, even from someone who may have recently suffered amnesia. "Yup, Robert, how did you know? We just suffered the first earthquake in the city's history. Aren't you glad to have been a part of it?"

"Julian?! I didn't see you there," Robert exclaimed, clearly startled by my presence. For some reason, he felt it necessary to cover his package, despite the fact he was wearing boxers. "What are you doing here?"

"Oh, you know, I just came over to see if you wanted to hang out," I said. I could see from the bewildered look on his face that he had no idea what I was walking about. "No, you jackwagon, we planned to meet up today. You were late."

Robert rubbed his eyes and looked at the clock next to his bed. "I guess I overslept. I'm just more tired than usual."

"Of course. How could I have forgotten that yesterday was Homeless Fest 2016? You were probably out til the wee hours of the morning. I'm surprised you're even awake now, to be honest."

"Very funny," Robert replied.

"You know what's not funny? The fact that I've had to wait to for your poor ass two days in a row."

"I'm *so* sorry," Robert said sarcastically (apparently he didn't know that was my bit). "Did Mr. Moneybags have to wait for a few a minutes? I can't imagine that type of injustice or suffering. It's a travesty! If I were you, I'd call the chief of police and have me arrested."

"Maybe I should. Or maybe I should stop paying for this motel room for you."

"Fine by me. I honestly don't give a fuck. I've slept on the streets for the last ten years, so it's not like I'm not used to it."

"Just put some fucking clothes on so we can go," I said, walking back into the living room.

I sat on the couch and waited for Robert. And waited some more. And then, waited even more. What the fuck was it with people making me wait lately? Their time might not be worth two pennies, but mine was valuable. I'd waited for girls on dates for shorter periods of time than I'd waited for Robert the last two days, which was saying a lot because the girls I took on dates were *very* attractive. And the more attractive, the longer they took to get ready. It was simple science. Of course, there was an exception that proved the rule true, and that exception was Robert.

Finally, after what felt like an hour, Robert walked into the living room. I'd like to say it was like one of those teen movies where the ugly duckling walked down a spiral staircase looking like the prom queen, but it was the exact opposite. Robert wore vibrant orange pants with a magenta Hawaiian shirt. My stomach was queasy just looking at him, but I managed to hold back the vomit.

I did not acknowledge Robert nor did he try to speak with me as we left the room. Fortunately, the full service salon was within walking distance, so we didn't have to deal with the rental car agency again, and we made our way toward downtown.

I waited for Robert to start bitching about his feet hurting or some other imaginary ailment, but it never came. He walked all the way to the salon in my preferred fashion. Silence.

The salon entrance was located in an alley, attached to the back of a K-Mart. In other news, K-Mart is still around. Anyway, I probably should have known from the salon's location that it was nowhere I wanted to be, but there was no one else willing to take on the 'special case'.

Needless to say, the salon was shoddily built. The building was decrepit, bricks were missing in several areas, and the sign was off-kilter by about thirty degrees. But that was nothing compared to the interior. Half the lights were dim, to the point that they were almost absolutely worthless. The ones that gave off more light than a fireflies ass flickered so obnoxiously that they would have caused anyone with epilepsy to have a seizure just by reading about them. A stained countertop stood alone a few feet from the door. A computer that looked like it was from the 1980's sat atop it. It was the kind of thing your grandmother would have purchased years ago to 'keep up with the times' but never had the technological aptitude to upgrade beyond. I highly doubted it could even access the internet. The floors were stained by various chemicals every few feet, every plant in the room was either dying or dead, and the rug in the front looked like it had been devoured by an eclipse of rabid moths. There was only one salon chair, and the leather was torn in several places, revealing the remnants of foam cushioning.

Immediately after we walked in, we were greeted by what looked to be the salon's only employee, which came as no surprise. The place looked like it hadn't seen a paying customer in months.

"Well look what the cat dragged in," a high, lispy voice greeted us. "A hot vanilla latte and Mr. tall, dark, and hopefully handsome under all...that." The stylist flamboyantly gestured at the disaster that was Robert. Wearing bright red lipstick, intricately applied makeup, and a red bandana to pull back hair, the employee playfully stroked Robert's arm. "Ooh, I hope you are handsome." Oh, by the way, the stylist had a dick that was almost assuredly bigger than Robert's. Did I forget to mention that?

Robert seemed flattered at first. I couldn't imagine how long it had been since someone flirted with him. The homeless man didn't exactly have my debonair. But then the harsh realization came over him. He violently ripped his arm away from the salon worker. The look on his face said it all. It looked like a mixture between horror, disgust, and, for some reason, constipation. Real attractive.

"Well I guess I don't need to ask which one of you is in need of my services," the worker started. "My name is Julia."

You've got to be fucking kidding me. Julia? Murphy's law had never been so applicable. Ever since I first encountered Robert, my life was a series steadily intensifying disasters, which had culminated (at least for now) in the fact that I now had to change my name. Because I couldn't go on living knowing that I was an "N" away from being a shemale.

"As you can see, you have your work cut out for you with him," I said.

"Looks like it. You don't need any work yourself, sweetheart?" Julia asked, flirtatiously.

"No, it'll just be my friend here today," I said, grinning at Robert's contempt.

"Oh well. More for him then. So what do we need done today?"

"Honestly, it would probably be quicker to just tell you what he doesn't need. He needs his hair cut to a reasonable length for a human, he needs his beard trimmed, a bath or two or three or twenty, a manicure, a pedicure, probably some full body grooming so he doesn't look like a werewolf's retarded spawn, a full dental replacement or at least a deep tooth cleaning if you can't do that, a facial - and if you could just do that over his whole body that would be helpful. And that should just about do it."

"That's no simple task. Luckily, you came to the right place. It's going to take some time though."

"Take all the time you need. I know you're the expert, but I might start with a hedge clipper or a small chainsaw for the hair and beard. Probably speed things up a bit."

Julia told me to come back in three hours to check on the progress. I walked to a nearby coffee shop to brainstorm the next phase of the plan. It would do no good to get Robert all cleaned up if we couldn't figure out a way to get to Carson Gorelli.

I sat at the damn coffee shop for the whole three hours, straining my brain for any ideas, but nothing came to me. It would be nice to just find another hacker. That would solve all my problems. Unfortunately, there was no tree (that I knew of) that sprouted hackers, and there weren't exactly a plethora of them advertising their skills on Craigslist. It turned out that hoping a new hacker would appear out of thin air before me was the most plausible idea I could come up with. My other ideas (traveling by floo powder, using hypnosis to convince one of the guards to let us in and tell us the location, and dialing a random ten digit phone number and hoping that whoever answered was either Carson or someone or who knew him) were, what some people would call, unrealistic. Defeated, I walked back to the salon to check on Robert.

"How's it coming?" I asked as I walked back into the salon.

"Nearly done," Julia said.

"So, I've been meaning to ask you. What's the next step?" Robert asked me. It was the first thing I'd heard him say since we arrived at the salon. He must have acclimated himself to Julia. He hardly even flinched when he was caressed awkwardly, though I could not see the scowl on his face as his chair was pointed away from me.

"I don't..." I started, but before I could finish my sentence, I heard the door open behind me. There was no way. Two customers in the same day? That must have been like hitting the lottery for this place. I turned to see who would be insane enough to walk into this barren wasteland. A man dressed in a brown uniform set a package on the counter and walked out. A delivery driver. And suddenly, I had a plan. "I have an idea," I said, turning back to Robert.

Before Robert could say anything else, Julia spoke up. "Voila. This is my greatest work. It may not be as eloquent as Michelangelo's *David*, but when you substitute shit for marble, you can't expect the same kind of masterpiece." She spun Robert's chair around to face me. My jaw nearly dropped when I saw him. But it wasn't the shocking transformation that had me taken aback. I finally realized why Robert looked so familiar. I knew exactly who he was.

Chapter 25

September 28, 2000

A shot of whiskey sat on the bar in front of me. I clinked glasses with the girl on the barstool next to me and threw back the shot. It burned as it went down, but for the first time, it was a good burn. I was drinking the good stuff this time. This was the start of a new beginning.

"Are you trying to get me drunk?" she asked, brushing my arm seductively. She was hot. Whew, she was hot. From her shoulder-length brown hair to her stunning hazel eyes to her perfect ass and breasts, there was nothing about her that didn't turn me on. I could tell from the way she drew the eye of every guy in the bar that her looks drove them all crazy, and I knew it pissed them all off that I was the one with her.

"Oh, I've got a lot more than that planned for you," I shot back. I held up two fingers to the bartender to signal two more shots.

"I think I like where this is going," she said, licking her lips as she finished the sentence. The bartender set two more shots in front of us. She picked it up and held it in front of her. "You know what you have to do for me before any of that happens, though." She drank the shot without waiting for me. I quickly followed suit.

"I wouldn't be here right now if I didn't intend on doing that. This is just the appetizer. That'll be the main course. And after that, we can have dessert together." She playfully smiled back and rubbed her hand up my thigh. It took all my willpower to stop myself from getting a boner. Without asking, the bartender set two more shots in front of us.

"So, tell me a little bit about yourself," I said. I didn't care, but I'd never met a girl that didn't like talking as much, if not more, than sex. What a fucking drag.

"Hmm," she thought. "Well I like music!"

"You do?!" I mocked surprise. "Do you also enjoy eating food and breathing oxygen?"

She took my remark in stride. "Shut up!" She exclaimed, playfully hitting my arm. "There's this great new song I heard. Let me sing it to you:

'Look at the stars,

Look how they shine for you,

192

And everything you do,
Yeah, they were all yellow.

I came along,
I wrote a song for you,
And all the things you do,
And it was called Yellow.'"

I was pretty sure my ears were bleeding. "Ugh, I don't know what the hell that is, but I never want to hear it again."

Again, she seemed unphased by my comment. "Don't worry, I won't hold your putrid taste in music against you." She winked at me. "Think it's about time to get out of here?"

"One more for the road," I said, holding up the shot. We both took our shots, and then I got up from the barstool. I headed for the door, but not before planting a passionate kiss on her lips.

I made the short walk back to my apartment in less than five minutes. It was a small place, way smaller than what I felt like I deserved. It was one of those tiny little one room apartments where you could take a shit, scramble some eggs, and watch the morning news all at the same time.

I took one step through the front door, passed through the living room, and ended up in front of my nightstand. There was only one item in there: a handgun. I put it in my waistband like I'd seen in all the movies. Unfortunately for me, none of those people had been skinny, white guys. The

193

gun slid from my waistband down my right pant leg and hit the ground hard. It probably would have discharged if I didn't have the safety on. But I was a responsible gun owner. I made the *arduous* walk to the other side of my bedroom to get the gun holster that I never thought I'd need. After a much longer time than I'd care to admit, I concealed the holster and secured the gun in it.

The whole process took a lot longer than I expected, but I arrived at my apartment ahead of time, so I was in no danger of being late. And I only had a few blocks to walk. Before I knew it, I arrived at my destination, an abandoned alleyway that was less than two miles from my place. Now it was time to play the waiting game.

By the time I got to the alleyway, it was late in the evening. Darkness had completely fallen over the city; there were hardly any street lights in the area and almost none of the houses chose to turn on their exterior lights. It was the night of a new moon, so any hopes I had of moonlight lending a helping hand were squashed. But darkness was my ally. A blanket of auburn and golden leaves covered the ground, most raked into large piles, though there were a few yards that looked like they hadn't been touched. The temperature was unseasonably warm for the early fall.

I glanced down at my watch: ten-thirty. He was late. He was never late. I ran every possible scenario through my head, but nothing made sense. Maybe he got held up at work. But what were the odds that this was the one night that happened? Maybe he got tipped off. But there were only two people that knew, and I was one of them. The other one was probably still waiting at the bar for me to tell her that I succeeded. There's no way she would have changed her mind. Maybe he had some other plans for the evening. This was a legitimate possibility, but it still didn't seem very likely. He'd never had plans any of the other nights that I watched him.

So, I waited. And waited. And waited. The minutes ticked away into hours. In what both felt like forever and no time at all, it was one o'clock in the morning. Not one person passed by the whole time. It was horrendously monotonous. I didn't bring anything to pass the time, so I was relegated to watching the alley for any sign of movement, but the most interesting thing I saw was a few leaves blow in the wind.

A loud crash broke the silence. I was so startled, I jumped a good six inches off the ground. I must have dozed off for a few seconds. I quickly glanced at my watch and saw that it was just after one, so I couldn't have slept for too long. The sound came from somewhere in front of me, so I walked up to investigate.

I treaded slowly, right hand tightly gripped on the handgun on my waist. Slowly, a shape came into focus. I tightened my grip on the gun, ready to draw at a moment's notice. My heart beat fast in my chest, adrenaline pumped through my veins. I drew deep breaths to calm my anxiety. Inch by inch, foot by foot, I made my way to the shape. Finally, it came into focus.

It was quite possibly the most anticlimactic moment of my short life. The shape was just two aluminum garbage cans, one of which had been knocked on its side. I didn't even need to continue my search to learn who the culprit was. It was obvious a pair of alley cats were responsible for the disturbance. Of course it was cats, the most fucking useless animals on the planet.

Disappointed by the cock tease, I returned to my original spot, a section of the alley behind a brick wall that gave me an excellent view of the street in front of me. That's where I knew he would walk. Despite the disappointment I felt about the cats, I was fortunate to be woken when I was. I didn't want to miss my opportunity. More than that, the short adrenaline rush had reinvigorated me. I no longer felt tired. I was energized, maybe too energized. I was not content to continue to stand in one place. I needed to move around. My natural reaction was to pace back and forth. At least that was my first thought. I did not want to give away my position, so I couldn't do that, at least not all out. I did, however, allow myself to take one step, pivot, and turn the other direction. I repeated that over and over and over again, until my stomach started to do cartwheels. That killed a whopping fifteen minutes.

I slunk to the ground, discouraged. All the planning, all the waiting, was it all going to be for nothing? I could always wait until the following day, but that wasn't like me, it wasn't in my DNA. I told myself I'd wait until three o'clock in the morning, just over an hour longer, though my optimism was at an all-time low.

It was a good thing I didn't pack it in when I gave up hope, because ten minutes later I heard what sounded like faint footsteps in the distance. It was still too early to determine who (or what) made the sound, but if it was another fucking cat, I was going to shoot it out of pure spite. A few seconds later, it became evident that it was not a cat. When I strained my eyes, I could just manage to see the silhouette of a man.

I grabbed the gun out of the holster and cocked it as silently as I possibly could. If I had thought ahead, I would have already done that, but no one can plan every detail perfectly. It must have been quiet enough because the footsteps continued forward without hesitation. As it drew closer, the same emotions came over me as when I approached the cats (I realize that sentence sounds weird out of context). Slowly, the figure came into focus, and there was no doubt; this was the man I'd been waiting for. The darkness swallowed the alleyway as I fired four shots in the dark. The man dropped.

I walked forward to assess the damage. It was so much worse than I could have imagined. There was so much blood. I moved closer to look at the man's face. It had a look of sheer terror. His head bled profusely. I couldn't believe what I'd done. Though I did not know his name at the time, I was staring at the lifeless body of Robert Tindall.

Chapter 26

I'd always thought the man I shot died. I couldn't see how he possibly could have survived. That single event had affected my life more than any other I could remember. It was the reason why I was so shaken up by Robert's ruthless torture of the fake Alex Bellavick. It was the reason why I hadn't touched a gun in sixteen years. And, mostly importantly, it had sparked the idea for my devious career.

I was paid handsomely before I shot Robert, though I would have been paid more if I reported back when the job was complete. I'd never had that much money at one time in my life, and I wasn't ready to give that up so quickly. And so, my devilish master plan was born. I would offer up my services as a hitman to anyone who I thought might be willing and who I could outsmart. After I got them to pay me half of the money, I would blackmail them to make sure they wouldn't do anything to get the money back. And in sixteen years, it hadn't failed me yet.

Somehow, I was able to hide my awestruck face from Robert. Or at least, I was able to play it off as shock at the incredible transformation he'd undergone. I paid Julia and left a hefty tip for the miracle she (he?) was able to pull off. When we were far enough away from the salon, I told Robert the details of my nascent plan. He was skeptical to say the least (so was I), but he didn't have any better suggestions.

We continued walking until we got to the local mall. We still had Robert's wardrobe to address. I bought him a suit at Men's Wearhouse. Though he would not need it for this part of the plan, I suspected he'd need one in the future. Normally, I went to a tailor to get a suit for myself, but there was no way in hell I was going to take Robert there.

After getting Robert's suit, we went to Madison Park to get him a decent pair of shoes. Somehow, I didn't think his handmade sandals would suffice. Madison Park was conveniently located just down the hall from Men's Wearhouse. I'd purchased all my shoes there for the last five years. I came there so frequently that I was always greeted by first name. This time, however, I was a helped by a new employee named Jimmy. I only knew he was new because he was the first salesman that hadn't greeted me by name in the last three years. I did, however, see him talking to the manager, Jericho, who seemed to be explaining the situation to the new guy. Good. Everyone should know Julian Donahue, or at least his alias, Sam Alterson.

There was a lot of work to do over the next two days. It would have been nice to have some help with it, but I thought it better to do it myself than to enlist Robert's assistance. I started with the uniforms. That was the easy part. The local party goods store had exactly what I was looking for. I grabbed dark green jumpsuits for us, a large for myself and a XXL for Robert. I would have gone even larger, but that was the biggest size they had. It was all uphill from there, though.

It wasn't just enough to have the uniforms. They had to be perfect. So convincing that no one would question their authenticity. I was not going to risk blowing this - for lack of a better word - 'mission' because of an oversight. Unfortunately, this was not as simple as one would imagine. While it was easy enough to find images of the patterns I wanted sewn onto the uniforms, finding someone willing to do the embroidery work was a different story. Something about copyright infringement or illegal criminal activity or something - I kinda tuned them out the second I heard a no. But since my middle school home ec sewing skills were fleeting, I was relegated to what was a nearly impossible search. If only there was a bigger black market for embroidery, but that was nearly nonexistent (oddly enough).

Only after spending an inordinate amount of time on this less than noble quest did I find someone willing to sew on the patches. Granted, she was a pawn shop owner/fortune teller/candle maker/whatever-other-random-task-you-needed-done-er, but at least she didn't ask any questions. And she only charged me ten dollars. It wasn't quite worth the four hours I spent searching, but at least now I knew where to get cheap, copyright-infringed embroidery work done.

In retrospect, I should have known that my embroidery kerfuffle (or embroidery-gate as I'd come to call it) would just be the tip of the iceberg. My final task would prove to be the most difficult, but also the most important. Without it, my plan had absolutely no chance of succeeding. The odds of success were dubious, even if executed perfectly, but without the last piece, failure was ensured. I needed to get my hands on a delivery truck.

Now I know what you're thinking: *Julian, you're a man of means. Why don't you just buy a truck?* While the former may be true, you don't become a wealthy man without having a certain amount of business acumen. And while I had no problem affording the truck, it was difficult to justify the price tag for such a risky endeavor. Still, I looked into it, just in case there were no other options. Unsurprisingly, the selection was almost nonexistent. I *couldn't* believe delivery trucks weren't a hotter commodity. I could only find one truck with the correct body style, though its price tag was egregiously high and it would need to be painted and have a logo put on it - which inevitably would lead to another embroidery-gate type situation (what was the deal with people having morals and wanting to obey the law?).

I did not dwell on the discovery too long, as the results were exactly what I expected. My next hope was to rent a truck. I had about as much confidence in that as I did in purchasing a truck. I was already hesitant because of my experience with the overly enthusiastic fuckstick who rented me the screaming metal death trap, but that doubt was doubled by a dearth of available options. At no surprise to me, I couldn't find a single agency that rented out delivery trucks. Apparently the demand to rent a delivery truck was even lower than the demand to purchase one. That only left me with one feasible option. Deep down I'd known it was the only realistic option, but I had to be sure before I could convince myself to go through with it. I was going to have to steal the truck.

I knew this task wasn't exactly going to be easy, but it wasn't like I was stealing an armored truck. The only things aboard these trucks were a bunch of shitty care packages and some made-in-China garbage that people bought on Amazon. Nothing that anyone in their right mind would want to steal. The security couldn't be that sophisticated. At least that was my hope. I really didn't have the slightest fucking idea what kind of security these trucks had.

My first thought was to hack into the computer system so that I knew where each stop was. That would allow me to plan exactly where the optimal place to steal a truck would be. Unfortunately, that took a certain set of skills that I did not possess. This was yet another time Trevor would come in handy, but no, that bastard had to get killed. Even from the grave, Trevor could piss me off. Instead, I had to do it old school.

I knew what that meant, though: I was going to have to rent another car. Yippitty fucking skippitty. That, however, went much better than expected. I was able to get a car without any difficulty or backtalk from the clerk. Now, I had to play the waiting game. Luckily, surveillance was an area that I excelled in. As much intel as Trevor was able to gather, it was always me who did the dirty work, catching people in compromising situations or gathering evidence of their betrayal to gain the upper hand.

My plan did have one unfortunate downside, however. I needed Robert's help. As reluctant as I was to bring him along, I had the sneaking suspicion this car rental company wouldn't be nearly as receptive of me abandoning one of their cars as certain other companies.

Robert and I waited outside one of the out-of-town exits that led to a small suburb. The fewer eyes on me, the better. I made sure that the car we rented had tinted windows, but I slouched way down in my seat and Robert sat in the back to ensure that I could not be seen. As far as any passersby were concerned, our car was just another one of the many that were parked along the side of the road. I prepared myself for what was sure to be an excruciatingly long stakeout, especially with Robert along.

We arrived at the exit around eight in the morning(and I'll be damned, but Robert was waiting for me on the corner). It was early - surely we would not see any delivery trucks pass by for several hours, but I knew the earlier in the day, the better our chances of success were. It would be easier to catch the driver off guard and more people would be at work.

"See anything yet?" Robert asked, ten minutes after we parked the car. Kindergarteners had more fucking patience than him. But I had a plan to avoid what I assumed was his new life goal of driving me insane.

"What's that? I'm having a hard time hearing you up here!" I spoke much louder than necessary to drive home my point.

"DID YOU SEE ANYTHING YET?!" Robert roared. Why did he have to do everything in the most obnoxious way possible?

"Still can't hear you very well! And to be honest, it's kinda distracting to have you yelling in my ear all the time. Maybe it would be best if we just focus on tracking a truck."

Robert, who had been leaning over the center counsel to try to make it easier for me to hear him, slunk back into his seat, a look of disappointment on his face. For a guy who most assuredly hated every fiber of my being, Robert tended to get bizarrely offended when I chose not to interact with him. Oh well, fuck him.

Content to keep to myself, I passed time by playing Angry Birds on my phone (fucking world seven, level nine was really kicking my ass). I snacked on gas station goodies and drank what was quickly becoming cold coffee. I'd even been kind enough to pick up some of the same for Robert. Fortunately, because of my insistence that we focus instead of talk, I did not have to listen to Robert bitch about the quality of the food. Though, in this case, I was inclined to agree with him. The food was like chewing through plastic and tasted about as good, while the coffee was watery, yet somehow bitter, with more floating grounds than I was comfortable with. Still, it was enough to keep me energized and focused on the task at hand.

Just after eleven o'clock, a truck finally drove by. I waited for it to get more than halfway down the exit before I pulled out. I maintained a safe distance so as not to seem conspicuous, but still remained close enough that I did not lose sight of the truck. It was a fine art, one that had taken years to master.

About a mile out of the city, the truck stopped to make a delivery. The whole neighborhood was bustling with traffic. Kids played outside and bored housewives gossiped with each other. There was no way I could make my heist there. So, I waited at the corner until the driver pulled away. The next stop was in one of those neighborhoods where all the houses looked the same and were situated about five feet apart. I thought this might be a good spot, but the driver was back in the truck before I could make up my mind. So, I continued pursuit. I followed the truck further away from the city for more than ten miles. The houses were becoming more and more scarce, the trees more plentiful. Finally, it turned off into a heavily wooded area with houses no closer than a quarter mile apart. This was it. It was now or never.

I parked around the corner and waited as the driver grabbed a package from the back. The second he was obscured from view, I darted to the truck, Robert taking my place in the driver's seat (I purchased the insurance this time - who knows what Robert would do to the car). I had to be quick if I wanted to remain unseen. I was prepared to hotwire it (another skill I'd developed in my years of practice), but was glad to see that the driver was foolish enough to leave the keys in the ignition. It was like he was asking me to steal it. If only he'd left it running, though. I'd never driven a truck like that before. It was not nearly as simple to start as I would have liked. By the time I finally figured out what to do, the driver was already walking out the door. I put the pedal to the floor and sped away as the driver chased after, yelling profanities.

I drove for about five miles, then pulled over at a dead end road. I searched the truck for a GPS or some sort of tracking device. It didn't take long to find; it was located just underneath the dashboard. I threw that, the driver's scanner, and his cell phone on the side of the road. With any luck, they'd track it that far and have no idea where I took the truck.

I didn't see any police cars on my way back, so I figured I was in the clear. At least for a while. The night before, I'd managed to find a garage for rent that was large enough for the truck. Robert was already waiting for me by the time I returned. The garage was located a few miles outside the city, but it was on the bus route, which we would have to use the next day (I would never let my sister live down the hell I had to put myself through to find her).

Chapter 27

Apparently, expecting Robert to be on time twice was asking too much, because I had to wait for him for more than fifteen minutes the next day. I will, however, give him credit for the fact that he didn't compound the anguish of riding the bus by talking. Though, I wasn't sure if that was a good omen or a bad one...

Robert and I quickly changed into our uniforms and climbed into the truck. Robert didn't even bitch that the color of the uniform didn't bring out the color of his eyes, nor did he find any other bullshit reason to complain. I should have known that was just the calm before the storm.

Less than a mile down the road, Robert turned to me, panting like a dog. "It's so hot in here. I'm sweating my ass off."

Really, Mr. Homeless? You stay in a motel for a few weeks and now you expect to live a lavish life of luxury? I didn't legitimize his complaint with a response. Bad choice on my part. If you're dealing with a chronic complainer, always head them off before they get a full head of steam.

Not even thirty seconds later, Robert was right back at it. "It's like a sauna in here. My ass is sticking to the seat. Did you turn the A.C. on?"

"It's on full blast," I said as I contemplated swerving into oncoming traffic.

Robert put his hand to the vents. "I don't feel any air coming out. It must be broken. You couldn't even get a truck with decent A.C.?"

"I'm sorry that the air conditioner wasn't exactly my basis for stealing a truck in broad fucking daylight, risking my life and liberty."

That shut him up, and neither of us spoke again until we got to Groveland Heights.

I'd envisioned Groveland Heights thousands of times, but nothing could prepare me for its splendor and majesty. I could hardly believe my eyes when we pulled up to the community. The houses epitomized wealth to excess, massive in size with elaborately-planned grand entrances, meticulous architecture, and perfectly-groomed landscaping. I could not see a single house without a swimming pool or guest house. For some people, this would be the true definition of delusions of grandeur. For others, it would be cause for envy and the reason tensions existed between the upper and lower class.

Not unexpectedly, we had to get through a guarded gate before we were allowed to enter the community. In fact, I'd been counting on this. We approached the gate and the guards opened it without hesitation. Before we entered, I stopped at the guard booth.

"What can I help you with?" the guard asked. He was a large man with a thick beard. He would have been intimidating to most people, but I could tell within seconds that he was a lover, not a fighter, more comparable to a teddy bear than a dangerous man. He had a gun on his belt that I doubted he'd ever shot.

"We've got a package here for," I feigned looking down at a notepad, "Carson Gorelli. It's just marked to Groveland Heights. It doesn't say the full address."

"You can just leave it here with me. I'll deliver it when I'm done with my shift." He didn't seem hesitant of us, but instead seemed to be acting on orders not to give out any information. Not to worry; I was prepared for that.

"Afraid I can't do that. It goes against company policy. If we can't deliver a package, then it has to get taken back to our facility and returned to the sender."

He looked over at the other guard for reassurance, which he received in the form of a nod. "He lives in the big house on top of the hill, on the right hand side up there. Can't miss it."

It was hard not to marvel at the houses as we drove past. They were even more exquisite up close. Even Robert looked to be in awe, though that easily could have been a look of disgust. His facial cues were never clear.

We got to the top of the hill and got our first glimpse of Carson Gorelli's place. The guard was right; we couldn't miss his house. Actually, house wasn't even the right word to describe it. It was less than a castle, but more than a manor. The main house was the brightest tint of white I'd ever seen, adorned with picturesque columns, the quality of which rivaled the Romans'. The two houses beside it were almost exact replicas, though without columns. On their own, they would have been considered mansions, but on this property, they were just guest houses. And I had the feeling that there were other guest houses that could not be seen from the road. The lawn was a luscious shade of green; it was the only grass I'd seen that compared to the country club. The cobblestone driveway that curled up to the main house was so well-taken care of that it looked as if cars were forbidden from driving on it. The were several marble and bronze statues in the yard, and two large oak trees bookended the property. I'd thought of Gorelli as simply a wealthy man, but it was clear I'd underestimated him. He took the definition of rich to a whole new level. Judging just by the estate, I guessed that he had amassed such an excessive fortune that at least five generations of his family would not be able to spend it all, even if they tried.

The contemptuous look on Robert's face gave away his position. Not that I needed the physical cue to know that he would be absolutely disgusted by Gorelli's exuberance and excess. As he surveyed the property, his hands curled into tight fists. His passionate hatred for the wealthy was akin to Hitler and the Jews, Republicans and Democrats, or Mr. Sanders and exercise.

As we walked to the door, a wave of anxiety swept over me. My normally high bravado was reduced to a mere wisp, replaced by nerves and apprehension for meeting the one man that might actually know the whereabouts of my sister, the man who might be behind all of this. But I had two big testicles, so I pushed those feelings deep down inside me and knocked on the door.

A man dressed in a gray button down shirt and freshly pressed black slacks came to the door a few seconds later. He bore a slight resemblance to the boy in the picture. I had no doubt this was Carson Gorelli. His gray hair was styled with gel and he flashed a toothy grin as he opened the door, though it was quickly replaced by a look of surprise. He studied the two of us, but he lingered a while longer over me. He seemed to be suspicious of our presence, especially me, but his toothy grin returned. There was no denying he was a handsome man, and that smile had surely won of the hearts of many girls. He would have made one hell of a wingman.

"How can I help you gentlemen?" he asked politely, almost charmingly.

"Are you Carson Gorelli?" I asked.

"Maybe. That depends who's asking." That was enough to confirm it.

"We're delivery drivers. I thought that was pretty obvious."

"I got that. But what can I do for you?"

I was beginning to regret the fact that I hadn't practiced what to say during our interaction. I'd spent so much time making sure that the plan went perfectly that I didn't even think about what I would say if we made it to Gorelli's door unimpeded. "Uh...we've got a package for you," I replied.

"It must be a really small package," he said. I suddenly realized that we'd walked to the door empty-handed. How did I not think to grab a package - any random package - from the back of the truck?

"We left it in the truck," I said. "We wanted to make sure we had the right place first. It was addressed to a..." I reached in pocket and pulled out a piece of scrap paper, "...Carson Gorelli, but the exact address was left off. Does he live here?"

He gave me a look like, *how the fuck do you know who I am*, but answered anyway. "He does. That's me."

214

"Good. I'm glad we found the right place. I'll run to the truck and grab it for you."

I walked back to the street, stopping by the cab of the truck first. I needed something to write with, a sharpie preferably, but I could only find a pen, so it would have to do. I grabbed a package at random out of the back and scribbled the name *Carson Gorelli* and *Groveland Heights* in my chicken scratch. Handwriting was never one of my strong points, and it was made even worse when I was in a rush. I hustled back to the door and handed the package to Gorelli.

He studied the package for a few seconds. "No return address, no stamp or shipping label." he turned the package over in his hands. "And I don't think my name is Barry dos Santos from Lake City." Sensing that we would not stop him, Gorelli ripped open the package. "Ooh, an Easy Bake Oven, exactly what my teenage boys have been hoping for." He tossed the package at Robert's feet. "Why are you guys really here?" he asked.

I turned to Robert, seeing if he had anything to interject, but he looked dumbfounded. Funny how he could boast for hours on end about the smallest triumphs, but didn't have anything to add in a tough spot. So, I continued. "We just want to talk to you. Give us five minutes of your time and this will all become clear."

"I'm a busy man. I don't have time for that." He slammed the door in our face without saying another word.

Robert and I stood on the front steps. I really should have planned that better, had something convincing that would make him want to speak with us. I walked down the steps and sat on the ground, putting my hands on my face in frustration. A few minutes later, Robert walked down. "Let me try to sneak in and have a word with him. I think I might be able to help."

That made me decide to forgo my forthcoming mental health evaluation. I knew I was insane because I agreed. "Whatever," I said. "Give it your best shot. I don't see how it could hurt things."

Robert walked around to the back of the main house. I couldn't see him when he turned the corner. I had no idea what he was planning on doing. I sat on the sidewalk, basking in the sun, rays beating down on the back of my neck. It was a hot day, much hotter than the average September day. I laid down on the sidewalk and shook my head. There was no way that Robert was going to find a way into the house and get Gorelli to agree to talk to me. I laughed to myself just thinking of the idea. It was comical. And then the door opened and I nearly shit myself. There stood Robert and Gorelli side by side. Gorelli motioned for me to come inside.

If it was possible, the inside of the house was even more extravagant than the outside. Paintings adorned almost every wall. And not those cheap paintings you find in a Michaels or some other craft store. These were real, opulent paintings, the kind you'd only expect to find in a museum. Everything about the house took extravagance to a whole new level. The staircase that led to the top floor was immaculate. The sides were made of a beautiful, opalescent glass, interrupted every few feet by bronze beams. Gorelli motioned for me to join him and Robert in the living room.

It was even more exquisite than the entrance. A leather L-shaped sectional sat in the middle of the room, directly across from what must have been at least an eighty inch television. Gorelli took a seat on the couch and offered us seats in the chairs across from him. He picked up a glass of whiskey from the table beside him and took a sip. "Can I get either of you something to drink?"

Robert gave a firm "no" without hesitation. I pondered the offer. Then, for the first time in my life, I turned down a glass of top shelf liquor. This was business and I wanted to be focused. I also didn't want to have to stay any longer than I had to.

"More for me then," he said, walking back to the wet bar to fill up his glass. "So, what is it that we need to discuss?" he asked when he returned. He looked directly at me when he asked. Gorelli knew I was the one calling the shots. But the way he looked at me gave away more than that. I had the feeling he knew exactly who I was.

I didn't want to waste any time beating around the bush, so I jumped right in. "Do the names Frank Davacchio or Dale Showen mean anything to you?"

For a moment, his eyes opened in surprise, in a sense of wonderment of how I knew those names. He quickly caught himself, though, and looked at me defiantly. "Can't say I know them. That Davacchio guy, he's the one running for Senate, right?"

"Yeah he is. But I don't think that's the only way that you know him. At least this picture would suggest otherwise." I grabbed the picture from one of the many pockets on my jumpsuit and handed it to Gorelli.

Gorelli chuckled indignantly. "You caught me. This picture is what...forty years old...that obviously proves I'm in cahoots with them. You're ridiculous. They're just some guys that I went to elementary school with. I didn't even remember that until you showed me the picture. I haven't seen either of them in decades." He was backpedaling. It was clear to me that he knew both of them. He just was not expecting that we'd have any real proof.

I stared at Gorelli, not buying into his bullshit. "It's funny, some people seem to disagree with that. People who are so intimidated by you that they've uprooted their family just to protect themselves." I was careful not to make it obvious I was referring to Alex Bellavick. I really didn't want him to end up like Trevor just because he agreed to help me, but I needed Gorelli to know that I wasn't just spewing nonsense. "You know, I'm surprised I didn't see you at Dale's party the other week. Were you busy or did we just miss each other?"

Gorelli stared at me defiantly, then his lips curled into an evil smile. "Can I have a word with you alone, Julian?" If there had been any doubt about his relationship with Frank Davacchio and Dale Showen, there wasn't any longer. I hadn't introduced myself and there's no way Robert would have mentioned my name. The only way he would know that is if he knew those two men.

Gorelli led the way out of the living room and into the dining room. A large wooden table covered with intricate designs took up the majority of the space. A glass display case showed a variety of tableware, the value of which surely was in the millions of dollars.

He put his hand on my shoulder like a father talking to his son. Which felt weird because I was no more than ten years younger than the man, and unless he was getting busy at *really* early age, that was impossible. "Look, it's not too late to do what you have to do. I'm assuming that since Robert is accompanying you, he has no knowledge of your task." I definitely was not going to tell him the truth, but I couldn't lie either. He'd see right through that. So, I remained silent and gave no indication either way. That did the trick because he continued. "You have to kill him. It's the only way you'll see your sister again."

"If you hurt her, I'm going to kill you and everyone involved."

"Better do what you have to do, then. Time is ticking." With that, he left the room to get Robert. I headed for the other exit, toward the front door, but something caught my eye before I left. A gold wall hanging of a coat of arms was situated just left of the door. I moved toward it to examine it more closely. It was the image of an Ouroboros dragon with swords piercing each of its wings . And in the center of it all was a diamond insignia with the same markings as Frank Davacchio's ring and Dale Showen's cigar case.

Chapter 28

The next day, I went back to the public library because I just wasn't doing enough to build my self-loathing. In reality, I needed to find out more about that damn symbol, and the library had significantly more resources than I did in my apartment, which, aside from Google, was nothing. That symbol had to have some kind of significance. It could not be a coincidence that three men I'd come in contact with had it.

So, I put on my big boy underwear, fought the urge to slit my wrists, and walked into the library. The moment I crossed the threshold, I felt the life sucking out of me and my soul ripping away from my body. It was the real world, inanimate manifestation of the Dementors from Harry Potter. And it was every bit as horrifying as J.K. Rowling described.

Adding to the *insurmountable* joy I was already feeling, I saw that the sweetest old lady in the world sat behind the desk: the peach of a librarian from the first visit Robert and I paid to the library. She didn't pay me any special attention as I walked in. Probably because she'd spent so much of her time yelling at people that no one stood out as particularly significant to her.

I walked to the back of the library, past the computer section, to the reference books. There was a never ending pile of books on old coats of arms, symbols, runes, hieroglyphics, and every other straw I could grasp at. I couldn't possibly look through them all in a lifetime, let alone a single sitting. I looked through as much as I could, trying to wade my way through tables of contents and hundreds and hundreds of pages.

I didn't make it very far before the librarian approached. "What?" I asked, annoyed. "Did I turn the pages too loudly?"

"What do you think you're doing?" she scolded.

"Looking through some books." I said, careful to whisper so she didn't have another reason to yell.

"What?! Speak up. I can't hear you."

"Well that's kind of a double standard," I started, in a soft voice, barely above a whisper, "If I talk too loud, I get yelled at, but if I talk too quiet, you can't hear me. It's a lose-lose for me." As I finished my thought, I changed the volume of each word, alternating between a whisper and my regular speaking voice. I hoped that might balance out.

It turned out my logic was about as flawed as it sounded. The librarian whacked her cane across the back of my knee. I crumpled to the floor in a heap. She was much stronger than her frail appearance indicated.

I was surprised she didn't yell at me for the groan I let out or for the sound my body made hitting the floor. I pulled myself up, making sure to stay outside of striking distance. "You can't touch the pages with your greasy fingers. You'll ruin the paper," she said, condemning what I thought was one of the few perfectly innocent actions of my life.

"How am I supposed to look through the books then? I forgot to bring my cotton handling gloves."

She swung her cane at me again, but this time I was prepared and deftly avoided the blow. She was clearly upset that she missed me, but she did not swing again (thank god). She did, however, scoop up the pile of books I still had to look through and began to put them back on the shelves. She didn't seem bothered by her fingers touching the books. I don't really know what she expected of me anyway. If I would have checked out the books, I would have touched them with my fingers and she wouldn't have been able to do anything about that. Unless they had some crazy policy that forbade checking out books, which would render the building's existence virtually useless. It wasn't like touching the pages was that bad, either. I could have jerked off between the pages of one of the books. That would have caused a lot more damage and may have warranted a cane-whack. And surely there are weirdos out there that did that. Maybe she should spend more of her time trying to catch them and less worrying about the people who obeyed the majority of the rules and followed the societal norms of not masturbating in books.

Seeing as I had no interest in earning another whacking, I stayed as far away from the books as possible, but I didn't want to leave empty handed, so I returned to the computers. If I would have known that I couldn't use the books, I wouldn't have wasted any time setting foot in this hell hole. I could have used Google from my place without putting on pants, and I could jerk off in the comfort of my own home like a responsible adult. I don't know why jerking off was on my mind so much. Probably because it had been almost a week since I got laid. I knew exactly what I was going to do when I got I finished at the library: get myself a one way ticket to pussytown. But first, I had to take care of business.

I sat down, stretched out my typing fingers, and began my work. I tried every search I could think of, using every possible variation of terms I could muster, this time even trying to include the coat of arms. Still, my efforts yielded no results. Each failure brought more frustration, which I took out on the keyboard, hammering the keys harder with each new query. That did not go on very long, as the librarian swooped over unbeknownst to me, slamming her cane on the table beside me. Once again, the irony was lost that her action was exponentially louder than mine.

"Be quiet! Are you trying to wake the dead?!" she bellowed from her seat at the counter. I assumed she was talking about her siblings. I ignored her and continued on.

My searches became more creative. Or maybe it was actually more desperate. Either way, my queries were nothing I'd considered before. I attempted to press the keys softer than an angel landing on a tempurpedic bed in a field after the first snowfall of the year. Still, my paranoia was higher than a stoner walking past the police station. My eyes constantly darted toward the librarian, and when she looked in my direction, I lowered my head so it was blocked by the monitor. Either she forgot I was there, was distracted by something else, or my stealth tactics worked because I managed to avoid drawing her attention. On the downside, that made the going a lot slower. Not that it mattered, though. I still couldn't find a whiff of information about that fucking diamond.

As I sat at the computer, my mind started to wander. I thought about everything. Dale Showen. Was he just a pawn in someone else's game? Frank Davacchio. This shit had to go deep to get a U.S. Senate candidate involved. And whoever was pulling the strings had to have some serious reach if they could absolve his blame or compel him enough that he was willing to risk everything. Carson Gorelli. How did he fit into the puzzle? He clearly was one of the major profiteers, but was he calling the shots? That diamond insignia that seemed to pop up everywhere. It had to have some significance, but what did it mean? Whether or not there might be someone else involved. As much as I wanted to believe that Gorelli was the mastermind, something told me this went above even him. And my sister. How could I have let this happen to her? The one thing in this world that I truly cared about. The one person that actually mattered to me. I even thought about Robert. As much as I wanted to believe that he was just another homeless man, I knew there had to be more to it than that. No one would be willing to pay $500,000 to have a homeless man killed just for sport. He was a target and there was a reason why. I never asked why I was meant to kill him the first time. I was young and naive, just doing it for the payday. The pussy was a bonus. I didn't know a thing about Robert, and the file Dale Showen had given me proved almost equally useless.

I continued my search, even daring to go through more than twenty pages of Google search results. And let me tell you, that's not somewhere you ever want to venture. The shit in those depths is not something you can ever unsee. It still scars me and it probably will for life.

I laid my head on the desk in frustration. Suddenly, the lights flickered and my head shot up. What the hell was going on? Was it just an electrical problem? A power surge? Something more? I rose from my chair, curious to find the cause of the problem.

I strode toward the front of the library. When I got in clear sight of the door, I saw it was just the librarian flicking the light switch up and down. Crazy old bitch. Before I could get close enough to ask what the problem was, she hollered, "Library's closed!"

I glanced around, but it looked like I was the only one in the library. I guess I was getting kicked out. But I was not planning on going easy.

I pulled out my phone. It was twelve p.m. "At noon on a Tuesday?" I asked. "You guys must have some pretty weird hours." I smiled with all the charm I could muster (admittedly, far from my best effort, but it should have been enough to work on her).

"Well, maybe I just don't like you. And today is a special day. We're doing inventory, so you're going to have to leave."

A library taking inventory of their books? Fat chance of that. There's no way they'd have any interest in knowing how many books had been stolen. But I felt my desire to fight back slowly slipping away. Truthfully, I didn't want to stay any longer. I just didn't enjoy being told what to do, especially by that wrinkly broad. But the idea of me openly campaigning to stay in the library? That was hysterical.

I walked out the doors of the library and down the long stone steps. The lights dimmed behind me. For a second, I could have sworn I heard the librarian cackle behind me like an evil witch. And as I got to the bottom of the staircase, I saw the light return to the building out of the corner of my eye.

Chapter 29

I desperately needed to find something out about the people that kidnapped my sister. I didn't know how much longer they would let her live. Carson Gorelli had tried to convince me that I should kill Robert, which meant she was probably still alive. But at some point they were going to realize that I had no intention of killing the homeless man, and then, that would be it for her. No, I couldn't let myself think about that. I couldn't let that happen. I had to get to the bottom of this. There must be something that I missed, some small piece of information that seemed insignificant at the time, but really was the key to finding my sister.

I quickly ran through all the facts again in my head. It was nice to have an outline of all the information I knew. It helped me to brainstorm some new search queries that hadn't crossed my mind. I sat in my comfortable leather computer chair and opened my laptop. At almost the exact second my browser opened, I heard a knock on my door. I didn't get too many visitors, so that was a bit strange. And the few I did get were almost exclusively females that came home with me after the bar to...you know (I'm talking about fucking in case you're too dim to follow along).

I opened the door less than a quarter of the way to see a tall man dressed in a blue polo and khaki pants. He was a few years younger than me, probably early thirties, with such a big smile that it couldn't possibly be real. No one was ever *that* happy. "How are you doing?" he asked, as chipper as I'd ever heard a human being.

"Not interested," I said, shutting the door on his face.

I went back to my computer, but before I was able to sit down, I heard another knock. That persistent bastard. I opened the door a quarter of the way again, not surprised to see the salesman standing there.

"My friend, you closed the door before we had a chance to talk."

This time, I did not bother expressing my lack of interest. I tried to close the door on him, so naturally he shoved his face between the door and frame. The sides of his face were squashed so that his lips looked like a fish and his eyes nearly popped out of his head. I enjoyed seeing him like that and would have happily left him that way, but he pressed his hand against the door and overpowered me.

"Hola, my friend, I do not believe we have met. My name is Juan Carlos Martinez Vasco de Mendez, but you can call me Juan Carlos Martinez de Mendez for short." He extended his hand to shake mine.

In case you couldn't tell from his name, ol twelve names was Hispanic, probably Mexican from the looks of it. He had jet black hair that was gelled and spiked up. He spoke with a thick accent, but his English was surprisingly good, much easier to decipher than Carlos Padilla.

"Look, buddy, whatever you're selling, I'm not buying," I said, hoping he would get the not-so-subtle hint.

Instead, JCMVdM pretended like he didn't hear me. "Wait 'til you see what I have in store for you. Honestly, I have no idea how you've made it this far in life without one of these."

As he spoke, his accent virtually disappeared. To the ordinary person, he would have merely seemed suspicious, but it was easy for me to see the truth. He was either a sleazy salesman (the irony of calling someone "sleazy" was not lost on me) or a conman like me. Either way, I had no interest in speaking with him.

"The door is right there. Don't let it hit you in the ass." I motioned for him to leave. Instead, he moved his whole body inside the door, so when I closed it, it trapped the two of us inside together. Apparently I wasn't clear. Maybe I should have said "get the fuck out of my apartment".

"I appreciate you giving us the chance to speak intimately mi amigo," he said, strategically holding his body against the door.

"That's not at all what I was..."

"Why don't you take a seat?" he said, motioning to my couch. I didn't move a muscle, instead continuing to stare him down with a look so harsh that it was like my eyes were piercing his soul. "You're welcome to stay standing. I actually prefer if you stay standing." Just to spite the bastard, I took a seat on the couch. "Sitting was my first choice." Since sitting and standing were both out, I took a knee on the ground in front of him. For a brief moment, JCMVdM looked flustered. He opened his mouth to speak, but couldn't seem to find the words. A single bead of sweat rolled down his face. But he quickly found his footing. "A very innovative position, my friend. That is proof that you are the perfect man for this product."

He was absolutely infuriating. I had to admit, though, he was suave. I suspected that his combination of flattery, smooth-talking, and aggressive tactics made him a very successful salesman. But none of that was going to work on me. Charming and preying on unsuspecting fools was my M.O.

JCMVdM began to speak animatedly, so much so that he abandoned his position against the door. I took the opportunity to casually open the door. As he continued to speak, I waited for my chance, completely ignoring every word out of his mouth. When he moved into alignment with the doorway, I gave a hard shove, and he tumbled through the door. I closed it and locked it behind him for extra security.

I went back to my computer, happy to be rid of the pesky salesman. I was just about to continue my search, when I heard the familiar banging on my door. *You've got to be shitting me*, I thought to myself. The guy would just not leave me alone. I ignored him, hoping that would make him go away. For a moment, I thought he'd given up. But that lasted about a six seconds, after which he banged on the door again, this time with much more force. I implored myself not to address the man and focus on my fact-finding mission, but the constant pounding was too much for me to handle. I stormed to the door, opening it just wide enough that my voice could pass through the crack.

"Look, Sleazy Gonzales, I'm not interested in your bullshit product. Now get out of here so we can both move on with out lives."

I shut the door without hearing a peep from JCMVdM and returned to my computer. I still had not managed to make it past the Google homepage. And apparently Lady

Luck had a grip on my balls again because the moment my ass touched the seat of the chair, the pounding returned to my door. He was a royal pain in my ass. I needed to get rid of him once and for all. Then a plan started to form in the back of my mind.

I opened the door, this time wide enough for him to walk in. Before he had a chance to start his pitch, I began mine. "I'm glad you came back. You've shown an extraordinary amount of resilience today." He seemed confused by my sudden change of heart, too baffled to speak. "You're not the only one who's selling something. I've got my own sort of miracle product, but I don't go door-to-door trying to sell it. I need to make sure that my clients are the right people. And you've proven to be the exact type of man I'm looking for." JCMVdM stood in awe as I spoke. Salesmen are always the easiest people to sell something to. "Fire. The wheel. Sliced bread. The cell phone. The morning after pill. Some of mankind's greatest inventions. But what could be next? Look no further than right here." All my years of bullshitting really came in handy. I had no idea what I was going to say, but I spoke with such conviction that even I wanted to hear more about this revolutionary product. "I'm going to forever change your life. Day-to-day activities will never be the same. All you have to do is follow me." I started for the door and JCMVdM's eyes gave me a look of wonder of where we were going, a question I was happy to provide the answer to.

"I just happen to have one on hand. It's in the trunk of my car." He seemed skeptical, but his curiosity got the best of him. Of course, I had no intention of leading him to my car, but he didn't need to know that.

I led the way through the hall to the stairwell. JCMVdM followed me down to the first floor. We walked toward the front door, but I stopped just before the security (yes, my apartment was lavish enough to have a guard), pretending to tie my shoe. JCMVdM continued walking, however, and went through the door, just as I planned. I stood up and walked over to the guard. "Don't let that sleazeball back in." To put the cherry on top, I walked to the door and waved goodbye at JCMVdM, just to taunt him.

I walked back to my apartment with a satisfied grin on my face. The front door locked when it was closed, and I knew the guard would not allow JCMVdM to enter. I had enough clout to ensure that. The only way he'd be able to reach my room now was to scale the wall. I wasn't ready to entirely rule that out, but I felt pretty good that I would never see him again.

I walked back to my computer to continue my search. I leaned back in my chair and wiggled my fingers as I prepared to type. Suddenly, the fire alarm went off. I walked to the kitchen, but I wasn't cooking anything. I went through every room, but couldn't find anything that would set the fire alarm off. I walked into the hallway and heard the fire alarm going off out there as well. A group of people from my floor were gathered, confused looks on all their faces. I recognized each, but didn't know any of their names. I'm not exactly the friendly neighbor type. I'm more like the creepy guy next door in Disturbia, minus the whole serial killer thing. There was a woman so neurotic that I doubted she'd ever find a guy crazy enough to make her his wife. I was pretty sure she slept in the pant suits she incessantly fawned over, a suspicion that only grew stronger when I noticed that not even an impending fire could make her change. The only thing that superseded her love of pantsuits was her pathological adoration of her cat, of which I'd only heard rumors. Next to her was a woman I'd only seen in passing a few times, but she had to be the bitchiest person on the planet, if not the universe. Every time I walked by her, she was on the phone yelling about something. My guess was that a good fucking would calm her down a little bit, but her bitchiness was matched only by an ugliness so horrible it was offensive. Her face looked like an evil witch's, crooked nose and hairy mole to boot, mixed with that of a longtime meth addict. Her body was so disfigured that it looked like she was battling severe cases of cerebral palsy and multiple sclerosis simultaneously. The Dreadful Duo or Putrid Pair or Vomit-Inducing Vixens (I'm still workshopping names for them) were talking to two jabrones, probably the only two men either of them had ever talked to. If the two men were flirting, they were either blind, dumb, or extremely desperate. If they were simply discussing the fire alarm or shooting the shit, they would be better suited talking to the walls they leaned against.

When it became clear that the alarms weren't going to cease any time in the near future, the group made their way toward the stairwell, as the elevators did not work when the alarm sounded. Reluctantly, I followed behind, but I maintained a safe cushion. The last thing I wanted to do was get wrapped into a conversation with those four freakazoids. As shitty as my day had gone, almost anything would improve it. Speaking with them, however, was on the short list of things that would make the shit pile grow.

When I got outside, I saw the vast majority of the residents of my building gathered. A fire truck was parked on the street in front of the building. Several firefighters stood amongst the group, asking questions about what might have set the alarms off and how bad the damage might be. From my brief observation, it seemed that no one had any helpful or relevant information. The firefighters, though, seemed worried about the possibility of a fire.

Just as the firemen began to seriously assess the situation, the psycho cat lady ran up to one of them hysterically screaming. "My baby! My baby's still inside the building! You have to help my baby!"

"Jesus Christ you left a baby in there! What room?"

"1027!"

The firefighter shook his head in disgust. "Some mother you are." He darted inside the building, muttering something about her being unfit and calling child protective services. Normally, I made it a point not to agree with any public servant, but in this instance I found myself on his side. If ever there was a time to hit a woman it would be then, but it wasn't my place, so I did nothing.

The disfigured, meth head witch walked over. "I don't think he knew you were talking about your cat." Of course that crazy bitch called a cat her baby. I had to be insane to think she was talking about a real child.

A few minutes later, the fire firefighter returned, exasperated. He held something in his hand, but I couldn't tell what it was. It was obvious it wasn't a baby, but the way he squeezed it in his hand made me think it wasn't a cat either. "I didn't find your child in there, lady. All I found was this."

He handed her the item, which she grabbed excitedly and embraced. "My baby!" As she she hugged it, she turned toward me and the object became visible. *You've got to be shitting me*, I thought. It was worse than I ever could have imagined. It appeared to be cat, but when she hugged it, I realized it was a stuffed animal. Sending a firefighter into a potentially dangerous situation to save a fucking stuffed animal was almost as worthy of a blow to the face as leaving a baby inside, and judging by the way the firefighter grasped his fist and grimaced, I could tell it took everything in his power to restrain himself.

When the other firefighters finished speaking with the residents, four of them geared up and entered the building. Four others stationed themselves by the fire hydrant, ready to battle the flames if they got out of hand. Ten minutes later, the firefighters still had not returned. The tension amongst the group rose with each passing minute. Ten minutes turned into fifteen. Fifteen became thirty. Finally, after forty-five minutes of listening to the materialistic complaining of the people I was unfortunate enough to call my neighbors, the firefighters returned, masks off. There was a fifth person with them, someone I didn't recognize. And the firefighters did not look pleased.

They walked over to the four men still stationed by the fire hydrant. As they drew closer, I could make out the fifth person. He was a teenager wearing a dark gray hoodie, pants sagging so low that every bit of his boxers were exposed. I shouldn't have been surprised to see that they were covered in images of Pokémon. His eyes were so bloodshot that I could barely make out any white.

"We caught this little shitbag smoking a joint. And he was so excited to tell us all about the *hilarious* prank he pulled."

"You should have heard him," another firefighter chimed in. "'Dude, how funny was it that I pulled the fire alarm, dude? You should have seen the way everyone freaked out and ran outside. It was some crazy shit, man.'" He used his best stoner voice as he spoke. It was almost too good. I suspected he'd had some practice with the Devil's Lettuce in his youth. I was tempted to ask what they did with the joint after they found the kid. After the day I'd had, a few tokes would do me a lot of good. This didn't seem like the right time for that, though.

The firefighter that spoke to the crazy cat lady walked to the front of the group of residents. "It seems this was all a hoax. Some young punk thought it would be funny to pull the fire alarm in the control room. You can all rest assured, we checked every room and there were no signs of fire. It's safe for you all to return to your apartments." As he walked away and the residents began to enter the building, the firefighter violently grabbed the the cat lady's arm and pulled her toward him. "If you ever pull that shit again, I will send you into the next real fire we face before the rest of us."

"What's wrong? Have I been a bad girl," the cat lady asked, trying to her best to flirt. It was one of the saddest attempts I'd ever seen, but I was sure glad to witness it.

"Yes, yes you have. And if I didn't have to deal with this punk stoner, I'd be having the police haul your ass off for obstruction."

That must have broken her because she contritely retreated. I watched as my neighbors filed back inside. I shouldn't have been surprised to see that people were pushing and shoving to get through the door with absolutely no regard for the safety of others. The elderly were shoved to the ground, violent elbows were thrown, and there may have even been a few nut shots. Ah, the community I lived in, where big screen TVs, iPads, and other material items were treated with higher regard than "loved ones". They had such an affinity for these objects that they were willing to injure their fellow residents just to get back to them a few seconds sooner. It was a *beautiful* commentary on the state of our society.

My neighbors' apathy was the vomit covered cherry on top of the shit sundae of my day. I couldn't bring myself to go back in there. I needed some time to clear my head and think. I'd made no progress on my search and a few peaceful minutes might be just what I needed.

I started down the sidewalk, not really sure where I was headed. A few minutes later, I received a text message. It read, *Check your mail.*

I hadn't realized that I'd subconsciously started toward the post office. Though I was anxious to find out what awaited me, I knew that I had no other option. The message had obviously come from Frank Davacchio or one of his cronies.

I kept walking, the brisk evening breeze brushing against my face. The sun had almost set, what stars could be seen through the city lights slowly becoming more visible. There was almost no one out on the streets, which came as no surprise to me. The streets of the big city were dangerous at night, but that didn't bother me. I wasn't scared of that. But if I was completely honest with myself, I was scared of something. I was scared of what the future might hold and what might happen to my sister if I didn't make every move perfectly. And even if I was able to find her, there was no guarantee that I would make it out alive. I wasn't going to kill Robert, and that choice might just get me killed. I saw how easily and brutally they'd murdered Trevor. There was every chance I could have the same fate. Compared to that, the streets seemed like a pretty good option.

Before I knew it, I could see the post office in the distance. I looked up at the skyscrapers where massive conglomerates resided, CEOs in their illustrious corner offices. They made me sick. As far as I was concerned, they were every bit as bad as I was. They took money from poor, unsuspecting bastards to line their pockets. The difference was, I admitted I was a scumbag.

As I walked farther, the buildings only got bigger. I slowed my pace, examining the exuberant buildings and exquisite architecture. As much as I loathed them, I had to admit, they had pretty good taste. Half a block down the road, I came across the largest corporation, not just in the city, but in the whole state. As I admired the building, my heart nearly stopped. There, at the top, was the diamond symbol I'd searched so long for.

Chapter 30

How could I be so oblivious? I walked past the building at least once a month. How could I not have recognized that the diamond insignia on the ring and the image in the coat of arms was the same as the Vindicta logo?

As tempted as I was to run home and research everything I could about Vindicta Neuroscience and Technology, I knew I must continue to the post office. Davacchio or whoever had sent me that message had obviously done so for a reason. I just had to hope it wasn't walking into a replay of the last scene in the movie *Se7en* (ignore the underlying implication of incest).

The post office was devoid of life, so I walked directly to my P.O. box. My heart pounded as I approached the box. I fumbled through my pockets, struggling to grab my keys. I took a deep breath and inserted my key. What was waiting for me on the other side?

As I opened the door, I breathed a sigh of relief. There were no boxes, no body parts. The only thing inside (besides a few insignificant pieces of mail) was a post it note with an address. I stuffed the note in my pocket and raced out of the post office.

Now, I was even more torn about how to proceed. Was it really worth it to jump through their hoops and follow this trail of breadcrumbs? Or should I begin working on a plan to infiltrate Vindicta? The right decision just might save my sister's life, but the wrong decision...I didn't even want to think about what that could mean.

I didn't waste much time debating myself. I'd never been one to suffer from indecision. I'd always trusted my gut, and it hadn't led me astray too often. And just like that, I knew what to do. The more I thought about it, the more certain I became. I only had one choice. I had to follow the address on the note.

I punched the address into my phone and found that it was less than a mile away. That was an easy walk for me.

As I began my journey, I couldn't help but think about what was waiting for me. What could Davacchio or his handler want me to see so desperately that they were willing to lead me right to it? Was it going to be another feeble attempt to get me to kill Robert? Did they even still want

Robert dead? Did they *ever*? Or was it possible that this was the location of my sister? As much as I wanted to believe that, I couldn't imagine them leading me to my sister unless she was...no, she wasn't, I couldn't even entertain that idea.

My thoughts carried me all the way to the address. Nothing I came up with seemed too plausible, and the harder I racked my brain, the more absurd my ideas. I was so engrossed in my thoughts that I didn't look up until I was fifty feet from the building.

For a brief moment, I thought I might be dreaming. But I quickly realized how stupid that sounded and shook myself out of that. There was no mistaking the building. It was the same place Robert led me when he was supposed to be taking me to his motel.

I wasn't ready to believe that could be a coincidence. I didn't have time to dwell on that, though. I raced inside the building. This time, my jaw dropped so far, I swear I felt it hit the floor. I really needed to start expecting the unexpected because this whole being completely taken aback thing was starting to get old.

The entire building was completely empty, except for a single file cabinet in the center. And who stood there, file in hand? Fucking Robert.

Once again, I'm not stupid. I knew that couldn't be a coincidence. I approached the homeless man so quickly that he didn't notice me until I yelled, "Robert, what the fuck are you doing here?"

"I could ask you the same thing." He hardly seemed phased by my presence. In fact, he hardly even looked up from the file.

"But you didn't. Now answer the goddamn question."

"Take a look at this," he said, handing me the file, clearly trying to avoid the question.

I didn't have time to dwell on whatever he was hiding, however, because I quickly realized why Robert wanted me to look through the file. The cover bore the Vindicta logo. It was time to get some fucking answers.

In an instant, I gained a surge of energy. As I leafed through the file, my heart raced in my chest. The first few pages were just background information about the company and financial reportings. I knew Vindicta Neuroscience and Technology was flush with cash, but this was off the charts. Their revenues were nearing one trillion dollars. What could they possibly be doing to earn so much money? I flipped back to the beginning of the file and read it a little more closely. It seemed that they did something with brain development, but most of the terminology was too difficult to understand, even for a learned man like myself.

I didn't need to worry about that, though. I scanned the rest of the file until I came to the Key People section. And wouldn't you know it, there were some familiar names. Dale

Showen was the COO, Carson Gorelli was the CFO, and Frank Davacchio was a Senior VP and Head of Legal. They were more important than I could have ever guessed. Not only were these three men key investors and significant shareholders, but they comprised the executive team and made decisions for the company. And listed right above their names was the most important person, the reason I was in the library right now, the reason for everything that had happened in my life for the last few weeks: Michael Doonsbury, CEO.

Unsurprisingly, I'd never heard of Michael Doonsbury. He'd gone through quite a bit of effort to stay out of the public eye, even sending his minions to do his dirty work for him. Clearly he was a man who didn't want to be found. But I found him. Well, actually, technically, Robert found him first, but he's just a footnote in this story.

I continued to look through the file and came to section that showed the blueprints of the building. The place was a fucking fortress. All the walls were reinforced with steel, the windows bulletproof. Security clearance was needed on every level, given by vocal recognition and fingerprint software. And there was only one entrance. If we wanted to get in, we were going to have to walk right through the front door.

When I finally set down the file, Robert turned to me. "So, what now?"

"It's obvious, isn't it?" I said, a grin spreading from ear to ear. "We pay a little visit to Vindicta Neuroscience and Technology."

Chapter 31

"I told you, we have to do this!" Robert argued.

"And the day that I start listening to you is the day I start sucking Lucifer's big, red dick," I shot back.

We stood in the living room of Robert's motel room. It was an absolute pig sty. Every other time I'd been to the room must have been after the maid service cleaned up. It was absolutely disgusting. Robert eyed me suspiciously as I brushed some of the paper off the table in front of me, but I didn't give two shits about the ramblings of a maniac.

"Stop pussy footing around like a ninnyrag. You know we need to."

We'd been having the same argument for close to an hour, and I was beginning to bore of it. We were both stubborn, but Robert needed to know that I was calling the shots.

"I'm in charge here, so we do what I say. If I wanted to buy a goddamn gun, I would have bought one and blown your brains out already and ended this a lot quicker."

"And I guess your solution is to just waltz up in there and pretend that we're all friends. Maybe you can get them to pinky promise that they won't kill you, and if you talk really nicely, they might even give you your sister back. By all means, bring your finger guns to the real gun fight. They seem like *reasonable*, *nonviolent* people with absolutely *no* tendency of killing."

Again, stealing my bit. Though as much as I hated to admit it, he brought up a good point. How was I supposed to know that we weren't walking directly into a trap. Doonsbury and his men were one step ahead of me the whole time. Who's to say they weren't expecting our visit?

I turned my back and started for the door. "Let's go."

"Where exactly are we going?"

"To the fucking gun shop." I didn't need to look back at him to see the smug look on his face. It cut right through me, piercing my flesh. If I ever agreed with one of Robert's suggestions again (God forbid), I'd have to convince him that it was really my idea. That shouldn't be too hard, considering who I was dealing with.

Seeing as gun shopping was not on my weekly to-do list, I let Robert lead the way. How he knew where to go, I had no idea, but I thought it better not to ask questions. He led the way across the city divide into the dirtier, more violent district.

For the life of me, I *couldn't* figure out why I didn't come to the area more often. Most of the masonry had deteriorated from the buildings, the sidewalk had more cracks than a plumbers' convention, and almost every window was barred. In this area, *I* was a minority. My suit and tie fit in about as well as Paris Hilton at a teen abstinence meeting. If I would have known that we were going to make this pit stop, I would have brought a change of clothes to better blend in, though I doubted that I would be able to truly pull it off. Even the newly made-over Robert stuck out like a sore thumb compared to the tattered jeans, do-rags, and exorbitant bling. Everything about this side of town made me cringe. It made the salon I took Robert to look like Buckingham Palace.

As we walked in the doors of Fully Loaded Gun Shop, the clerk behind the counter eyed us suspiciously, which was unwarranted. If anyone was a danger to the store, it was him. The man wore camouflage cargo pants and a Confederate flag bandana. He had a gun holstered on each hip, *just in case* he got attacked by two people at once. On second thought, if it could happen anywhere, it would be here.

He crossed his arms as we walked up and down each aisle, intermittently flexing each arm. I learned years ago that this was douchebag sign language for "don't fuck with me". Real effective tactic, buddy. It was difficult to keep a straight face each time I glanced at him.

After we'd gone through each aisle twice, I turned to Robert. "What exactly are you looking for?"

"A gun," he replied, so matter-of-factly that I almost felt stupid asking the question. Almost. But I knew who the fucking idiot was.

"Really? You mean you're not looking for a new skin lotion?" I shot back. "No, you fucking idiot, I meant what type of gun. In case you haven't noticed, they have a *couple* options here." There must have been over two-thousand guns in the store and Robert looked perplexed at the sight of every single one of them. "You don't have the slightest clue what you're doing, do you?" He didn't answer. "Let's just ask that salesman. He looks like a knowledgeable gun enthusiast, not just a radical right-winger who's trying to compensate for his tiny penis." Again, Robert said nothing, so I took that to mean to yes.

As we approached the counter, the man changed his silent tune and began to flex both arms as much as he could. His face started to turn red, but he continued. I was tempted to see if his bravado would persist long enough that he passed out, but that might hinder his ability to help us. Plus,

I wanted to get going. The sooner we got to Vindicta, the better.

"Hi," I said, "my friend here and I would like to purchase a gun."

"You know I have the right to refuse service to fags if it's against my religion."

"First of all, you couldn't be more fucking incorrect. That's not true. Second of all, we're not fags. Third of all, if we were fags, do you really think I'd be with this guy?"

After that, he completely reversed his course. And by that I mean he actually offered assistance, but still continued to be a royal douchebag. "So, what can I do for you peckerwoods?"

"Customer service really is your strength, huh?" The man had no business acumen. Technically, I was in the business of customer service as well. I spent hours, sometimes days, wooing my prospective clients. After I buttered them up enough and got them salivating for my services and in a position to be blackmailed, then I started to act like the asshat that I really was. That's the difference between someone with business sense and a bigoted hick running a store.

If I knew anywhere else in town that sold guns, I would have gladly walked out, but that wasn't the case. Besides, it would ruin the opportunity to teach the bastard a lesson.

"What the hell would do you know about running a business? You're just some punk in a cheap suit."

"I sure hope your brain is filled with information about guns because the rest of it is filled with hot air. This suit cost more than your car. If I wanted to, I could take your store, your house, and everything that you own. All I need to do is snap my fingers and you'll be out on the streets, not a dime to your name. Now, if you want to stop being a prick, we'd like to buy a gun. Otherwise, I will snap my fingers."

"What exactly are you gentlemen looking for?" I could swear I saw a tail between his legs as he spoke.

"He told you. We want a gun." Of all the things for Robert to say, he had to chime in with that golden nugget. Before this was over, he was going to give me an aneurism.

"I meant what kind, you stupid buffoon." I let that comment go. That was about as nice of a reply as Robert deserved. Personally, I would have gone with something a little more cavalier. "We've got just about anything you could want. Handguns, shotguns, rifles, whatever your heart desires."

As much as I wanted to continue to let Robert make a fool of himself, I jumped back in. We were burning daylight. "We need something that's easy to conceal. Something that packs a punch with a big clip."

"That narrows it down quite a bit, but I've got a few options for you." He walked through the aisles, returning with half a dozen guns. "We've got Glock, Smith & Wesson, Sig Sauer, Ruger, Kahr, and Beretta."

"That's sounds like the worst law firm ever," I said.

The salesman was not impressed with my answer. Even less so with Robert's. "Either that or the wordiest punk rock band name." Humor was clearly not his forte.

I decided it best to change the subject. "Robert, why don't you test one out?"

He picked two of the guns off the table and held them above his head like a cowboy in a cartoon. "How cool do I look?" he asked. He pretended to shoot the guns, even making a "pew, pew" sound with each 'shot'.

"What the hell are you doing? Stop that!" the salesman said, clearly impatient with Robert.

"It's fine. I have it under contro..." Before he finished the word, Robert got a little too careless and fired two shots into the ceiling, sending two ceiling tiles crashing to the ground.

"God damn it. I told you." He shook his head in disbelief. "I wish I could say that was the first time that's happened." I looked up at the ceiling. There were more garbage bags covering holes than there were actual ceiling tiles. "You'd be surprised how many people get a gun in their hands and think they're Yosemite Sam."

"You could just take the bullets out of the guns," I offered. "That might solve some of your problems."

The salesman pretended like he didn't hear me. "Here, try this one." He handed me a gun. "It's not loaded."

It had been more than sixteen years since I held a gun. It was heavier than I remembered. I pointed the gun at the counter in front of me and pulled the trigger. Before I could process what happened, the glass beneath the wooden countertop shattered.

"I thought you said it wasn't loaded!" I yelled, my ears ringing.

"I didn't think it was. Even so, why would you pull the trigger?" the salesman retorted.

"Because you said it wasn't loaded!"

"Even if a gun is loaded, you never pull the trigger unless you're willing to shoot what's in front of you. Don't you know the first thing about gun safety?"

No, I thought. *Actually*, my history with guns was more troubled than Dick Cheney's. In five lifetime pulls of the trigger, I shot a man in the head four times but somehow didn't kill him, and shot the glass out of a display case. I decided to keep this information to myself. Expressing my track record probably wasn't the best way to get a gun.

"Let's just take these to the back. You can shoot them off back there and you won't be able to ruin anything else." Boy did he grossly underestimate our ability to perpetuate chaos.

He led the way through a dusty hallway into a makeshift shooting range in the back of the store. There were four shooting lanes, each divided by a long wall of plywood covered in pages of *Mein Kampf*, separated by quotes and signatures of history's most noted racists. You know the type. Hitler. Andrew Jackson. George Zimmerman. Dummies hung at the end of the lane, each different. The first was painted black with tattoos and a flat bill cap; the face of the second was crudely colored with a brown marker, a purple turban atop its head and fake bomb strapped to the chest,; another had a sombrero and a goatee; the last one was covered in pictures of presidents, the word *Democrat* spray painted in blue over the top. Together, the four targets represented the four enemies of the most radical of the radical Republicans. This guy was seriously deranged.

Robert and I took our places, a table between us, on which sat all six guns. None of the lanes were particularly appealing, but the terrorist seemed justifiable, so I stood there and watched Robert. He picked the Mexican, grabbed the nearest gun, and fired six shots down the lane. It was difficult to see where they hit because the dummies were riddled with so many holes, but it looked like three hit in the head and the other three hit in the chest. I never pegged Robert for a good shot, but clearly I was wrong.

"That's pretty good shooting. For a nigger," the salesman said.

Robert turned to me, a look of contempt in his eyes so strong I thought he might put a bullet in the man's head on the spot. "Tell this inbred, sister-fucking, illiterate, hillbilly that if he calls me a nigger one more time, I'm gonna shove this gun so far up his ass, that he'll be able to taste the metal as I blow his brains all over the ceiling." While staring the hick in the eyes, he blindly fired three shots into the dummy, each piercing the figure's head.

Holy shit. I had to admit, I kind of liked feisty Robert. The salesman was so flustered he couldn't form an intelligible response. Finally, he gathered his composure, though he curiously stood behind a stack of boxes, as if he was trying to hide the lower half of his body. I suspected that he wet his pants and wasn't overly excited about the idea of either of us seeing the proof.

"Ah, pretty boy," the salesman said, stammering, "could you kindly ask that ni...friend of yours to wait outside?"

The manhood he so triumphantly paraded around evaporated. Robert had seen to that. I had to admit, when he was cleaned up, Robert could be pretty intimidating. His large stature coupled with the fire that was still lit in his eyes would be enough to make most men shake in their boots, which was literally true for the salesman in his cowboy boots.

I didn't have to say anything to Robert. He made his way to the hall, a big smirk on his face. When he was gone, I turned to the salesman, who still stood behind the boxes. "I think we'll take that gun."

"Bring it upstairs. You can just leave the others down here. I'll finish you up at the register. And do me a favor. Take the clip out before you go up there. I don't need any more damage to my store."

It was a fairly reasonable request, everything considered. By the time I got back upstairs, the salesman was already safely behind the counter. Unfortunately for him, he forgot that I shot through it earlier and even before that it had been made of glass. I bent down to 'tie my shoe', I got a full frontal of his piss-covered pants. The spot was so large it gave Lake Superior a run for its money. In an even more unfortunate event for him and a *very* fortunate event for me, the man turned around. Normally I'm not into checking out dudes' asses, but I couldn't help but stare at the brown stain located suspiciously on his ass. Ha! Behind his facade of masculinity, the salesman was just a little bitch.

I managed to stifle a laugh as I stood up. "So, we'll take the gun and a box of ammo. What does that bring the total to?"

He punched some buttons on the cash register, waited as it whirred and made its calculations, then finally it spit out a total. "After tax, it comes to $984.38. If you want to take it home today, I'll just need to see your ID and permit to carry a concealed handgun, otherwise we will start the three day waiting period."

"Good joke. Now here's $1,000. Keep the change for that, ah, little incident earlier." I laid a wad of hundred dollar bills on the table.

"I'm sorry, sir, but I can't sell you a handgun without a permit unless we begin the three day waiting period." There wasn't a hint of jest in his eyes.

"Really? That's where you draw the proverbial moral line? You make the Klan look like a kindergarten tea party, but you can't sell a gun to someone without a license?"

"No, sir. I can't do it. I've had the ATF up my ass for months. If they find out I sold a gun illegally, they'll take my shop away. I'd be happy to sell you something else, though. Rifles don't require a permit or waiting period."

I knew he wasn't lying, but I grew tired of him. And I hated not getting my way. Admittedly, I was a bit toddler-like in that manner, but I'd grown used to getting what I wanted. Everything had a price. But first, I needed to show the salesman that I was sick of his shit. "If I wanted people to know I was carrying a gun, I'd wear an NRA hat, drive a big pickup truck with a 'Don't Mess With Texas' bumper sticker, maybe get me a pair of them fancy overalls, and talk with a southern accent like the rest of you backwoods hicks."

I did my best southern accent as I finished my little speech, which wasn't very good, but it got the point across.

The salesman didn't have a rebuttal. I laid a few more bills on the table. "What if I sweeten the pot a little? Say $2,000?"

"Sorry, can't do it."

I laid another stack of cash on the table. "How about $3,000?"

"No, siree. Nothing doing here."

I laid even more cash on the table. "$4,000. Final offer."

"I'd be happy to take your $4,000...if you come back with a permit or in three days."

I stared at the man, purposefully pausing for dramatic effect. "You're really not very good at this whole sales thing, are you?" I didn't wait for the man to respond before continuing, though he seemed like he was trying to formulate something. "The $4,000 was so I didn't have to inconvenience myself by waiting or getting a fucking permit." I remained calm as I spoke. In my many years of dealing with the shitbags of the earth, I'd learned that strong words, delivered in a mellow tone were far more effective than yelling or losing my temper. "Not that I really give a fuck because there's no way in hell I'd actually go get one, but just out of curiosity, how long does it take to get a permit?"

The salesman jumped at the chance to answer, like he'd been waiting all night for me to ask that question. "To process all the paperwork and receive your permit in the mail, it usually takes around three months, provided you have the proper training."

"Three months? You've got to be fucking shitting me. Is this a new season of Punk'd or something?" I plowed on because it looked like the salesman wanted to interject. Man, he really didn't understand what a rhetorical question was. "How can it take three months? Isn't it in the constitution that we have a right to bear arms? Why does it need to be bogged down by all the bureaucracy?" Smart move. Appeal to his 'ultra-conservative, fuck the liberals, protect the constitution at all costs' side.

"That's what I'm saying. Give the people back their rights!"

"You know how you can fight the tyranny that the liberal establishment has imposed on us law-abiding Americans?" Again, the stupid fuck opened his mouth to answer. Didn't they teach anything in the South besides how to shoot a gun? "You sell me a gun. Maybe your next shipment is a little light. It's a win-win. I get my gun and you get $4,000." The man paused, scratching his head, clearly pondering something. "I take it that means you're thinking about it?" I asked.

"No, I was just trying to think of another way to say no to you. As much as I like the offer, I can't sell you a gun without a permit."

"It looks like my business here is done. Thanks for the collossal waste of time." I turned toward the door, but stopped about half way across the store. "You really aren't very good at business." He didn't seem to like where I was going, but for once, he kept his mouth closed. "I gotta ask you one more question. "Why did you open your business here? Why didn't you just stay in Texas where they let kids sell guns at their lemonade stands?"

The salesman flashed me a big grin, revealing all eight of his remaining teeth. "Come on, you should know the answer to that. Pussy."

I shook my head, a grin spreading across my face. What men would do for a good piece of pussy. I turned back toward the door, but couldn't bring myself to leave without making one more comment. "Just so you know, you've got piss and shit all over your pants. Might wanna clean yourself up before your next customer walks in."

Chapter 32

Robert was waiting for me right outside the store. He leaned against the brick wall, fiercely scribbling in his notebook like always. When he saw me, he hastily shoved it into his pocket. "Where's the gun?" he asked, when he saw that my hands were empty.

"I ran into a little bit of trouble with that. Did you know that you need a permit to purchase a handgun in this state or else you need to wait three days?"

Robert sighed and shook his head. "Stupidity is a sin, but ignorance is a far greater sin."

"Look Robert, I don't have time for your bullshit riddles and cryptic babblings. So why don't you save us both some time and say what you've got to say."

"How do you not know the gun laws of the state that you live in?"

"I don't know. Maybe because I'm not a big purchaser of guns." If I was ignorant, he definitely fit the bill for stupid. "I don't go out every morning for coffee and then stop at the gun store to pick up some heat."

If Robert was the expert on the state laws, why did he lead me to a gun shop? He had to have known that I was clueless, especially considering how adamantly I was against getting a gun in the first place. But he didn't bother to respond to my comment. "Now, do you have a solution to this gun problem or are we going to go with my plan without a gun?"

Again, Robert grinned, but this time it became more of a smirk. I didn't like that look. "I think I might have an idea."

Robert led us on what could only be described as a wild goose chase, orchestrated by two chickens with their heads cut off and feet walking in different directions. First we went to a super store that looked like it hadn't been in business for ten years. There were a few cars in the parking lot, but not a person in sight. Almost immediately, Robert declared it was the wrong spot. Next we stopped at an abandoned warehouse with the roof caved in. There were a few people outside, all of whom either looked like they were on drugs or were interested in buying drugs. Robert surveyed the crowd, but decided this wasn't it either. After that, we went to a pier. All the buildings were at least partially destroyed, damaged by fire, by the looks of it. The water was so murky and black that I guessed even dipping one toe in would lead to poisoning and eventual death. Once again, Robert decided this wasn't the right place. I was beginning to think Robert didn't know where the hell he was going and he was simply leading us around for his amusement. I decided to give him one more shot before I called the search off.

Robert walked up the decaying stone steps to a basketball court. Despite their less than fortuitous nature, the steps were in better condition than the court. At one end, the hoop laid on its side, as if it were removed from the ground. On the other end, the hoop sat at a forty-five degree angle. The backboards had chipped away to virtual nihility. What remained of the chain net had rusted to a deep maroon color, and even that looked like it barely clung to the rim. A suspicious car was parked on the sidewalk parallel to the court.

"This is it!" Robert exclaimed. We must have been looking at two different things because I couldn't believe he actually thought this was a place we could buy a gun. Still, he continued across the court and approached the car.

As we got closer, I saw that the interior of the car was completely packed. From floor to ceiling, the car was covered in loose clothes, empty fast food bags, and even a pillow and blanket. "Uh, Robert," I began, skeptically, "how did you say you know this guy?"

"Let's just say we used to hang around a lot of the same places," Robert said.

"You mean he's homeless?"

"Semantics. All you Americans worry about is semantics and the meaning of words. Words are such fickle organisms. In context..."

I didn't have time to inform him that he, too, was American, but I needed to head him off before he went on another wild tangent. "Hey, hey." I snapped my fingers in his face. "How about we stay on task?"

"As I was saying, he wasn't really homeless. I mean, he didn't have what most people would call a home..."

"That sounds pretty homeless to me," I interjected.

"Let me finish. Anyway, he may not have had a home, per se, but he didn't have to sleep on the streets or in shelters like the rest of us. He had this sweet ride to sleep in."

Robert slapped his hand on the trunk of the car. The sad part was, Robert wasn't being sarcastic. He genuinely thought the car was something to look at. Though to him, it probably was. He probably hadn't owned a car in decades. Hell, I bet aside from the car we took to the party, the first car he rode in in years was the shitbucket that we rented to drive upstate. He probably thought that was a sweet ride too.

"So he's a gun dealer who can't turn enough of a profit to make a rent payment. He must be really good at his job."

"If you thought that last guy was a regular Al Bundy, wait until you see this guy. And he has a bit of a habit that seriously cuts into his profits." Great, so we were dealing with a man who was probably so high he didn't even know which way was up. Which would explain his less than exceptional business prowess. He sounded like a real standup guy.

Against what I would have advised, Robert approached the driver door of the car. He knocked lightly at first, but that wasn't enough, so he pounded more violently. The guy was either a really heavy sleeper or in a drug coma. Or a real coma.

The man who got out of the car looked nothing like I imagined. His hair stuck out at angles that even science couldn't explain. His nose was so crooked it must have been broken a half dozen times. With a gaunt face and pale skin, he could have easily been mistaken for a vampire, though he did have a reflection. I checked.

I didn't have a lot of experience with drug addicts besides Trevor (with whom I had a strict 'no drugs while I'm in the building' policy), but I'd seen them on TV and in movies. I always thought their portrayal was just another Hollywood over-exaggeration, but this man was the spitting image of those characters. When his arms weren't aimlessly flailing like Michael J. Fox in the evening, his whole body shivered.

"Julian, this is Clay," Robert said. I wasn't big on giving out my name, but this tweaker was so fucked up he probably didn't even know what year it was. I'd say his chances of remembering my name tomorrow were right up there with my odds of winning the lottery, getting struck by lightning, and banging a fatty in the same night.

"What, ah...what can I...what can I do for you guys?" Clay asked. As he spoke, his head continually darted from left to right. Whether that was because he was paranoid because of the drugs or the weapons in his car or because he was hallucinating, I had no idea.

"Well, Clay, we were hoping you were still in business. We'd like to make a purchase."

Clay lurched his head and shook it, like a high school student trying to stay awake in class. "Huh? What?" The guy was so out of it I wouldn't be surprised if he passed out standing up.

"The guns, Clay. Do you still sell guns? We want to buy one," Robert said.

"Guns?" Clay said it like he'd never heard the word before.

"Jesus Christ, you meth head. You're a gun dealer. Now can we buy one or not?"

"I'm not a meth head...anymore. I've moved onto better things. I do heroin now, which is only sometimes cut with meth." The first coherent thought he could form and not even on fucking topic. How did this crazy bastard survive this long in life? I'd never been so upset about Social Darwinism's failures.

"God damn it, Clay. Open your fucking trunk and get us a gun."

Clay did not react. He stood against the car, mouth agape. I'd never seen Robert so upset. His eyes had a fire in them, even more than at the gun shop. Robert stormed over to Clay, dug his hands in the druggie's pocket, and yanked out his keys.

Beneath the random hodgepodge of shit (blankets, ropes, and for some reason dog toys?), were four guns. Not an overwhelming selection, but desperate times. Robert picked one up. "This one looks alright. Julian, what do you think?"

"Whatever gets us out of here the fastest."

"Sounds like we're going with this one then."

"Clay, what do we owe you?" I asked.

Clay blinked his eyes like he didn't hear me. But then, in a slow, monotonous tone he said, "$4,000."

"$4,000?! Are you fucking nuts?!" I couldn't believe he had the audacity to charge such a ludicrous price. I understood that there was a premium for black market goods, but quadruple the retail price was akin to robbery in my books.

Despite the fact that Robert hadn't been in the gun store earlier, even he knew that the asking price was more than unfair. "I'll handle this."

Robert marched over to Clay, gun still in hand. I'd never seen Robert look like that before. He'd been upset with the gun store owner, but this was different. His face was full of rage, his eyes full of hatred. He looked like a completely different person.

What transpired next seemed to happen in slow motion. It was like I knew what was going to happen before it happened. His right foot lifted off the ground. Then his left. And then before I knew it, it was all over, and Robert stood over the cold, dead body of Clay, a bullet wound in his head.

Chapter 33

"Did you huff paint when you were a kid?" I asked Robert.

"What?"

"Do you have early onset dementia?"

"Huh?"

"Did you suffer a severe head wound?" You know, other than the bullets that may or may not still be lodged in your brain.

Robert gave a weird look before responding. "I understand the words you're saying, but they don't make sense when they're arranged in that particular order."

"I'm just trying to figure out what the fuck could have made you lose your mind and do something so impulsive and utterly moronic." Fuck, I would have gladly paid the guy

$4,000 if Robert would have have let me get a word in. I may not have been happy with his markup, but that was just the businessman in me coming out. Everything could be negotiated and it was in my DNA to get the very best deal possible.

Did he think anything through? It was like babysitting a child, except more sadistic and violent.

"Calm down." Robert reached out his hands, motioning for me to simmer.

"Calm down?!" I slammed the trunk of the car with all my strength, but, being a piece of shit, it bounced back up, the latch broken. "How do you expect me to be calm when you just murdered a guy for no other reason than he was *there*?"

"I had a reason. He was trying to rip you off."

"Awe," I said, feigning sincerity. "I didn't know you cared about me so much. Let's braid friendships bracelets and get matching tattoos so we can commemorate this joyous occasion."

Robert looked at me and shook his head. "Why are you getting so worked up about this?"

"Oh, I don't know. Maybe because I don't want the fucking cops on our asses as we walk into one of the biggest and probably most secure companies in the entire fucking country." Our task was going to be difficult enough without the police looking for us. But Hasty McDumbfuck didn't stop to think about that.

Much to my surprise, Robert chuckled. "You rich, white people have such a distorted view of the cops. They don't care about what happens in the poor communities. They won't care about the death of a homeless man. Even if they find his body, they'll probably just chalk it to suicide so they don't have spend their time investigating it."

"Don't try to worm your way out of this." I wasn't going to let him feel like what he'd done was justified, but he was right about one thing. If you needed police assistance in this area, you were better off calling a cab to take you down to the station than wait for them to respond. I let my brain focus on that so long that I almost skirted over the most important thing he said. "Wait. What do you mean *if* the police find his body?"

If he hadn't just murdered someone, this might be the craziest thing Robert had done all day. I know Robert and I had a penchant for ill-advised plans with even worse results, but this had to be one of the worst yet.

"I'll back the car up to the building, then you put his body inside the car," Robert said.

"No fucking way am I touching that body," I argued. "You killed him, you can move his ass. I'll move the car." I was up for some pretty sick shit (several ladies can attest to that), but I drew the line at dead bodies.

Surprisingly, Robert didn't bitch about my unwillingness to move the body. Even he was sane enough to realize it was his problem to deal with. I backed the car up to the building because Robert insisted that we needed to get a full head of steam. He was full of antiquated statements like that, which *really* were a pleasure.

When the car was in place, Robert started to drag the body over. He was so much larger than Clay that moving the body was as easy as moving a rag doll. He put Clay in the front seat of the car and fastened the seatbelt.

"Is the seatbelt really necessary?" I asked. I admit, they do save lives, but Clay was already dead. Safety was probably not at the top of his list of concerns.

"We need to make it look legitimate," Robert replied.

"Oh yeah, that's right, I forgot that a lot of people with bullet wounds in their head drive themselves into the water."

"Just...just find me something heavy." It gave me great pleasure to know that I could fluster Robert so easily.

I found a small boulder beside the building and handed it over to Robert. He placed it on the gas pedal. That's when his plan started to go wrong. As soon as the large rock touched the gas pedal, the car went backwards and slammed into the building, breaking through the thin, aluminum siding.

"Damn it, Julian, why did you leave the car in reverse?"

"Maybe because I didn't want the car to fly into the water without the body." Again, Robert didn't fight me, so I was two for two.

Robert trudged into the building and switched the car into drive. We watched as it drove into the water, slowly sinking. Then, my worst nightmare happened.

While at least half of the car was still visible over the surface of the water, a police car pulled up.

"I thought the police didn't care about what happened in the ghetto," I told Robert.

"Shut up," Robert said. I think I was starting to hurt his feelings. Not only that, but Robert looked anxious. He could hardly keep still.

"Just be calm and follow my lead," I said.

As the officers exited their car, I started toward them. Robert seemed skeptical about my approach, but he did not voice his concerns.

"Officers," I said, greeting them, "what brings you out here this fine afternoon?" I looked up and saw the gray clouds coating the sky on one of the most overcast days in recent memory. Hopefully they didn't notice that.

"Oh yeah, it's beautiful," the officer from the driver seat said. There goes that. "Makes you wish every day could be this beautiful. Forget sunshine and blue skies. This is heaven on earth."

He was a short, graying man, with a stomach so large he looked to enjoy the cliched doughnut eating a hell of a lot more than the problem solving portion of his job. His partner, a black man with a medium build and thin mustache, could not help but laugh. It was tough for me to keep a calm demeanor as well, but it was imperative I did.

"You're right, Officer," I leaned in and dragged my finger across his nametag, "McClellan. Those days are overrated. It's days like today that remind you that you're still alive."

"That's one way of looking at it," the black officer said cracking a smile. His nametag read *Stearns*. The irony that the two officers were the mirror opposite of Robert and me was not lost on me. The black man was the well-spoken debonaire officer and the white man was his much uglier, more abrupt counterpart. Even after his makeover, Robert was the lesser man compared to me.

"What exactly are you guys doing here?" the white officer asked. His tone was cold and abrasive. If only he knew me.

"It just seemed like a *beautiful* day for two gay gentlemen to stroll through the park. Isn't that why you guys stopped here?"

The officers obviously were not expecting that answer. Officer McClellan tried to stutter through a coherent thought, but Stearns gained his composure more quickly.

"Well then, I don't suppose you'd mind if we took a look behind you. That building over there has a pretty good sized dent in it. Looks like vandalism to me."

"Or maybe a little B&E," McClellan said, trying to sound like a big shot.

"Relax, I don't know if we need to go bothering any judges to get a search warrant." He was smart, much more so than his counterpart. "But, I don't think it would hurt anyone if we took a little look around."

I could feel Robert exuding panic beside me. We couldn't let the cops walk over to the water. There's no way the car had sunk yet. We needed to stall, and since Robert was going to be about as helpful as sunblock in a snowstorm, it was up to me. "What's the matter? Sick of talking to us already? I thought the small talk was delightful."

The vein in Officer McClellan's forehead stuck out so far it looked like it was going to explode. He moved so close to me, I could feel his spit on my face. "Listen here, you little punk. What do you say we throw both of your asses in jail for contempt? That oughta wipe that smug little smile of your face." He punctuated each sentence by jabbing his finger into my chest, spit flying from his mouth at the end of every word.

I backed away, mainly because I'd showered earlier that morning. But there was more than that. I knew McClellan's threat to throw us in jail was just him trying to show us how big his dick was, but if he poked my chest one more time, I wasn't going to respond very nicely and that would almost certainly earn us a one way ticket to a jail cell, which was not an option.

"Ugh, have you ever heard of breath mints?" I retorted. "And if you're going to get that close to someone's face, you might want to warn them to get an umbrella first." It physically pained me to make a joke that excruciatingly dimwitted, but I had to keep my humor at an infantile level so I didn't go over that imbecile's head.

McClellan advanced, ire exploding in his eyes, but Stearns held out his arm to force his partner back. "I'll handle this," he said. He moved closer, but maintained a safe distance, so I was in the *no fly zone*, so to speak. "Is there some reason we shouldn't be looking around here? Something you're hiding?"

"Does that little number ever help you get intel? Maybe try dancing a little jig next time. Maybe then you'll get the information you so desperately crave." The look on his face clearly said he was not interested in, what I would call in my unbiased opinion, my sharp wit. "Now, back to the matter of looking around. It's a free country, officer. You can look around wherever you'd like."

The officers walked toward the warehouse. Hopefully that would keep them occupied for a while. Robert and I trailed behind. Robert was still shaking in his boots, literally and metaphorically. I assured him that we would be fine, so long as we were able to stall for a few minutes, but it was like everything I said went in one ear and right out the other. I couldn't squelch his fears, and if I wasn't able to soon, he would give us away.

"Well, well, well, what do we have here?" Officer McClellan said. I wonder how long he waiting to whip out that old cliche. He moved closer to the building and banged his fist on the wall. "This is a pretty good dent. It would take something pretty big to make it. I'm thinking: four wheels, a windshield, and maybe some taillights." He paused a second. "I'm describing a car, in case you're too thick to catch on."

I hated him almost as much as I hated Robert. There's a sentence I never thought I'd say. He thought I was smug, but so was he, just in a different way. He was the kind of guy who thought he could say and do whatever he wanted because he had a badge. That kind of shit doesn't sit very well with me. "Looks like you caught us red handed. Robert, why don't you hand your keys over to this *fine* officer of the law. Here's mine."

I tossed my keys in McClellan's general direction, not being particularly careful to let him catch them. "What the hell is this?" McClellan asked.

I walked toward the abominable officer. "They're keys. You're really not very good at this whole cop thing, are you?" I stopped just outside the splatter zone. "You've got my keys, now you've got the proof you need to arrest us for this heinous crime." I held my hands in front of me waiting for the handcuffs. "Oh wait, that's right, I don't have a car and that bastard couldn't even afford a Hot Wheels car."

McClellan was taken aback for a moment, but he wasn't going to let up that easily. "Or maybe you guys got rid of the car. You know, ditched the evidence."

Maybe I underestimated McClellan. He was smart, and he sure as hell wasn't going to go down without a fight. But neither was I. "So what, you think we abandoned the car in some junk yard? Or drove it into the water? All because we crashed it into some abandoned building. I have to ask, is it a prerequisite to join the force that you have to be a lunatic conspiracy theorist or do you just have to be a moron?" It was a gamble, telling the officer exactly what we did, but I was betting he would never follow through on the lead. Robert, though, was less certain. He shot me a look that clearly said, "shut your fucking mouth before I shut it for you". What a sweet sentiment.

Unfortunately for us, the officer called my bluff. McClellan slowly made his way to the water. I wasn't sure if enough time had passed for the car to sink, but I sure as hell didn't want to find out. I'm usually one to stay even-keeled, but my heart raced with each step he took. I racked my brain, trying to think of anything I could to slow him down, but I came up empty handed. Of course, when I needed it most, my propensity for thinking on my feet failed me. Twenty more feet and we were history. Ten feet. Five. Just as I thought my heart might explode out of my chest, a call came in on Stearns's radio.

Stearns listened intently, then swiftly responded, "We're on it."

Just before he got to the edge of the water, McClellan turned around. One more step and he would have been able to see the car. "What was that about?" he asked his partner.

"Armed robbery in progress. Tenth and Freedom. We need to get there right away. Come on. There's nothing to see here."

McClellan looked like he wanted to put up a fight, but he kept his mouth closed. He took one last look at the water, then he and Stearns walked to their car, but not before giving Robert and me a suspicious look, trying immensely to scare a confession out of us. Against all odds, if Robert was able to remain composed for a few seconds, we were in the clear. I could have sworn time came to a screeching halt as McClellan's piercing glare rested on Robert. He must not have seen the guilty look he so desperately craved because the officers exited the scene without another word.

Thank Jesus, Buddha, Allah, and all the other Gods (real and fictional) for getting us out of that mess. Normally, I wasn't much of a spiritual person, but if it was going to benefit me personally or help me bed a hottie at the bar, I was willing to set my thoughts aside.

Chapter 34

The next day, I met Robert bright and early. He was standing on the sidewalk when I arrived, and limited his complaints about the early hour from the usual one-hundred-fifty-seven to ten, a new personal low. Next and only stop: Vindicta Neuroscience and Technology.

The lobby was immaculate. With marble-tiled floors, a matching white desk, pretentious paintings, and a large fountain in the center of the room, it resembled the lobby of a five star hotel more than that of a massive corporation. The only person in the room was the receptionist behind the desk.

"We're here to see Michael Doonsbury," I said, flashing a grin.

"There's no one here by that name," she replied so quickly it was almost like it was rehearsed. She didn't even bother to look up from her computer.

The receptionist wore a stunning blue dress, which perfectly complimented her lustrous auburn hair. She probably had a beautiful smile, but currently her look was one of pure annoyance. Her glasses not only gave her the look of intelligence, but also a great deal of sex appeal. If I owned a company, I would *definitely* want her working for me. Hell, I contemplated starting a company just for that opportunity. Joking aside, if all went well, this could turn out to be a better day than I ever could have imagined. I could get my sister back and nail the receptionist and (hopefully) be rid of Robert forever. If there were complications, I'd settle for the last item. If you think that sounds callous, it's only because you don't know Robert.

I leaned in closer, ready to lay the charm on thick. "Would you mind checking again for me, sweetheart?"

The receptionist's annoyance turned to pure indignation. Again, she did not say anything. She punched a few things into her keyboard, then turned her monitor in our direction. "This is the entire employee directory. As you can see, there's no one named Michael Doonsbury here."

I scanned the entire list, but it was clear the receptionist was truthful. There was no Michael Doonsbury on the list. Still, something told me that she wasn't being entirely forthcoming. She knew who Michael Doonsbury was, and she likely knew that he was somewhere in the building. I needed a new approach.

"What about Carson Gorelli, or Frank Davacchio, or Dale Showen? Do any of those three work here?"

"You just saw the entire employee list, so you should know that none of those three work here either, unless of course your eyes don't work."

After she said that, I lost all focus on my mission. I only had one thing on my mind. "You're sassy. I like that. When are you getting off? And when are you done with work?"

"You're way out of your league, hotshot."

A challenge, huh? It was like she was trying to tempt me. Unfortunately, I didn't have time to keep seducing her, so I laid it all on the table. "As much as I'd like to stay and keep playing these games, I have some business to attend to. Once that's taken care of, we can get out of here and I'll take you on the wildest ride of your life."

She swiveled her chair and for the first time faced me. "I'm afraid I'm going to have to ask you to leave. If you refuse, then I will be forced to file a sexual harassment charge against you."

I wish I could say that was the first time I'd been threatened with sexual harassment charges. In my experience, most of the time those were empty threats, used to get me to leave, but the receptionist's face told me I didn't want to stick around to find out. Her scowl coupled with the anger in her eyes gave her the appearance of a vulture hovering over roadkill, just waiting to swoop in and claim the delicious prize.

I looked at Robert, but *shockingly* the cunning and guile that he was all too happy to brag about had failed him. He had no idea how to proceed, much less form a coherent sentence. We were at the metaphorical fork in the road, so to speak. The left fork led out of the building, but it also meant forfeiting what could be our one opportunity to get my sister back. Unfortunately, the right fork was covered by some brush and surrounded by a dense forest, so I had no idea where it led, let alone began.

Just before I was about to tell Robert that we should give up and regroup later, a voice from behind us said, "Put your talons away, Cindy. They're with me." Enter right fork.

The voice was clearly male, but it sounded strange. I had no idea how long it had been behind us. We would have heard if anyone got off the elevator and we would have seen if someone had walked down the main staircase. As far as I could tell, those were the only two entrances. It was almost like he materialized out of thin air, and the way things were going the last few days, I was almost ready to accept that as a possibility.

The man behind the voice was handsome, but short. His features were slightly effeminate, but he exuded confidence and power, so I doubt anyone had ever mentioned it to him. He wore a suit almost as nice as mine. Or maybe it was nicer. But I would never admit that. There was no doubt in my mind: the man before us was Michael Doonsbury.

"Follow me, gentlemen."

He turned and walked toward the wall behind him, not seeming to have any particular destination in mind. He stopped in front of the wall, though it soon became clear how he appeared out of thin air. Doonsbury deftly pressed a square on the wall and elevator doors opened up.

There was only one button inside and Doonsbury pressed it. I have to admit, I was a little jealous of his private elevator. That was something I definitely needed to look into.

Needless to say, the tension made the ride up deliciously awkward.

"So, the weather outside has been crazy lately," Robert said, trying to break the tension.

"Robert Tindall: master of conversation," I said to Doonsbury.

"He really can be quite annoying, can't he?" Doonsbury said.

"Tell me about it."

"I can't imagine how you've been able to bear spending so much time with him. Now you know why I hired you to kill him."

"Believe me, I wanted to a time or two...hundred."

"I'm right here, you know," Robert said.

Doonsbury and I exchanged a grin. I hated the man, hated him for the hoops he'd made me jump through, for the suffering he put my sister through. But all that aside (which was an awful lot to put aside), he was...well...likeable. As much as it kills me to say it, if we were meeting under any other circumstances, we might even be friendly acquaintances (I didn't have any real friends, nor did I want any).

When we reached the floor, the elevator doors again opened out of the wall from seemingly nowhere. A grand desk sat on the far side of the room, constructed out of exquisite ebony wood, ornate carvings trimmed the top. A brown, leather chair sat behind it, so enormous that the man sitting in it would exude the power of a Greek God.

Behind the desk, a bay window ran the length of the wall from floor to ceiling. Presently, the blinds were opened, flooding the room with more natural light than the fixtures on the ceiling could provide.

"This is quaint," I said, trying to lighten the situation. "You'd think with a company this size, you'd get a whole floor."

Doonsbury turned to me and grinned. "I know you speak in jest, but this room is just my office. I've got a conference room on the left that's almost twice this size. On the right, a bigger room yet. I don't really have much purpose for it, other than to say that I've got a room with more square footage than half the houses in this country."

Doonsbury walked behind his desk as he finished speaking. When he turned and sat in his chair, his expression intensified. Gone were the friendly face and endearing smile that had made me start to waver in my opinion of the man, replaced by indignation and a roaring fire in his eyes. This was the look of a ruthless, cold-blooded businessman who was used to getting his way. And when he didn't, someone had to pay. That someone was me.

"Have a seat Mr. Donahue. I believe we have some matters to discuss."

Chapter 35

Doonsbury immediately dismissed Robert, just as I would have done if I was in his position. But seeing as I wasn't, I was more than content to allow Robert to stay in the room and listen to the conversation. It was always more gratifying to insult him to his face. Doonsbury may have been raised to bite his tongue in someone's presence and whisper behind their back, but I at least had the decency to show my true colors to a man's face.

"Julian - may I call you Julian," Doonsbury started. I nodded. "Julian, let me ask you something. Why have you been so adamantly against killing Robert? He's a homeless man with no family, no one who cares about him. No one would miss him if he was gone. More than that, no one would notice. You were paid handsomely, more than I suspect you've ever been paid for any other job. Yet, still you refused. So I upped the ante to prove that I wasn't fucking around. I killed your associate. Yet still, you felt no urgency to kill this worthless man. So I had to go further. I kidnapped your sister and held her hostage, thinking that might be the only thing to call you to action. However, you still resisted, instead choosing to spend your time trying to track me down. Why go through all this trouble just to save Robert's life? It can't be because you genuinely care for the man; no one is that foolish. Please, explain this to me."

It was a good question, and one I'd contemplated many times. I could have ended this all by putting a bullet in Robert's head. Truthfully, I'd be doing the world a service. There were good people who brought joy to the world and happiness to people's hearts. And then, there were people like Robert who spread misery and chaos everywhere they went, always bringing down those around them. He was reckless and impulsive; he killed a man less than twenty-four hours ago. I didn't doubt that the world would be a better place without him. But even after all that, I couldn't bring myself to do it. I'd hardly been able to live with myself the first time I shot Robert. Admittedly, I thought he was dead, but I didn't know if I'd be able to survive that kind of trauma again. But that wasn't what I focused on when I responded back to Doonsbury.

"Other jobs? What makes you think I've had other jobs?" I asked.

Doonsbury grinned and shook his head. "Please. You should assume there's nothing I don't know about you. You make a living posing as a hitman, then use the information you gather to blackmail your 'clients' into letting you keep the money. Who else knew that you had a sister, much less that you would do anything for her, anything to keep her safe? I'm sure you don't tell that to all your golf buddies down at the country club. Yes, Julian, I know about that, too. I'm sure you don't tell any intimate information about yourself to the little sluts that you bring home from the bar. Do any of them even know your real name? You see, Julian, I know everything about you. And I've been one step ahead of you this whole time. Think about it. I mean really think about. How did you make it this far?" Doonsbury paused, letting his words sink in. "It doesn't add up, does it? You've had some amazing strokes of luck, found out some crucial pieces of information when all hope seemed lost, all of which led you to your next bread crumb. Did you really think those were all just coincidences?" Again, Doonsbury paused for effect. He wasn't quite on Robert's level, but he was really starting to get annoying. How could anyone think that every word out of their mouth was so profound? "They weren't. Robert's been mine this whole time."

I stared at Doonsbury defiantly.

"You don't believe me, do you? No matter." He raised his voice. "Robert, can you join us for a moment?"

A few seconds later, Robert walked back into Doonsbury's office.

"Thank you," the man who was slowly becoming my arch-nemesis (Robert was now a close second) began. "Could I borrow your journal?"

I could tell Robert was conflicted. In all the time I'd known Robert, I'd never seen him without the journal in his possession. It was like his security blanket. Begrudgingly, he handed it over.

Doonsbury leaned in and whispered something that I couldn't hear. When he finished, he announced, "That'll be all." Robert left the office again.

That simple act had been enough to convince me that Robert really had been working for Doonsbury all along, but Doonsbury insisted on reading from the journal.

Chapter 36

What Doonsbury read in Robert's diary was both shocking and unsurprising at the same time. It was completely in line with the enigmatic, paradoxical madman who betrayed me.

*   *   *   *   *

I'd been standing on the corner for nearly two hours. Yet I didn't have a damn thing to show for it. Not one of the greedy bastards that passed by could spare a dime. Most of them either ignored me or said they were too busy. More like too self-absorbed to help anyone but themselves. Not that I wasn't used to it, though. I'd lost track of exactly how long I'd been homeless for, but I knew it was close to a decade. In all that time, I'd never managed to get more than twenty dollars in one day. And even that came from one generous person. Most days I came up empty-handed, left to fend for food entirely myself.

The rest of the morning continued the same way. My bucket was still empty. After about an hour a man approached. He was different than most of them. He was sharply dressed, wearing a full suit, hair neatly trimmed, carrying a briefcase. He looked important, looked wealthy. I'd never gotten so much as one cent out of someone with money before. They were always too busy or didn't see the point. I always found it a bit ironic that the rich people - the ones that could more than afford to spare a few dollars - were never the ones to give money. It was always the lower or middle class people, the ones that could relate to me, maybe even people that had been in my shoes once upon a time.

"Not your best day," he said, peering into my empty bucket. His voice sounded deep and masculine, but forced, like he was trying to sound intimidating. Or maybe he was overcompensating for some endowment problems.

"And you're not making it any better."

"I bet you get a lot of people to give you money with an attitude like that."

"Oh, so you're one of those?"

"One of what?" he asked.

"A jackass that just came over to gawk at me and tell me about all the mistakes I've made."

His response caught me off guard. He chuckled. "You're right about one thing. I am a jackass. But that's not the reason why I'm here."

"Then why are you here?" I almost didn't ask the question. I thought I knew the answer and I didn't want to hear it. Aside from people lecturing me about my missteps, the next most common reason for people approaching me on the streets was to tell me about Jesus. You know those naive, self-righteous, born-again people that think all your problems can be solved by turning to God? They were so humorous to me. I was really supposed to believe that all of my problems could be solved by putting my faith in some old, bearded guy who lives in a cloud? That doing so would somehow help me get out of poverty and into prosperity? And I bet if I wished hard enough and really believed that I could win the lottery, too, right? They both seem about equally likely.

"Actually," he began, "I was hoping you'd be able to help me with something."

"If you're looking for a donation, you might want to try somewhere else."

"No, no, nothing like that," he said, smiling and shaking his head in disbelief. "What do you say we grab lunch and discuss this a little more?"

I thought about the offer for a moment. At another time in my life, I would have been skeptical. Why would a random stranger offer to buy me lunch? And why did he want my help? That raised more than a few red flags. But what did I really have to lose? A whole lot of nothing. And what was the worst that could possibly happen? He'd kill me? Not like anyone would care or even notice. No one had for the last ten years and I don't know why anything would change now. And I can't say I'd be too opposed. I no longer had anything to live for. Still, I proceeded with caution.

"Tell you what, I'll make you a deal. You can tell me about whatever it is you want from me right here, and then I'll have lunch by myself, just like I do every day."

"If you would prefer that, then that is what we'll do." He paused, choosing his next words carefully. "There's a man, his name is Julian Donahue. He's become sort of a problem for me. I need you to make sure that he finds his way to me."

"And how exactly am I supposed to do that? Lead him right up to you? Why would he trust me?"

"He wouldn't. You just leave that part to me. Your job is just to make sure that he doesn't lose focus and stray from the path and maybe help him out a little bit. If you do that, he'll find his way to me."

"That's it? That's all I have to do?" I asked. It sounded too easy. There had to be a catch.

"That's it. I don't need much. Just a shepherd to guide the sheep to pasture."

"And what do I get out of it?"

"You didn't think I'd forget that part, did you?" I did not respond. "Of course I wouldn't. If you're able to do this for me, then I'll make sure that you never have to be on the streets begging for food again. I'll make all of this go away."

That got my attention. As unwilling as I was to accept that kind of charity, I'd be a fool to pass that offer up. This could change my whole life. "So all I have to do is take some guy to you and you're going to give me a place to sleep and food to eat?"

"It's as simple as that."

Every bone in my body screamed that this was too good to be true. I'd be insane to believe that someone would trade so much for doing so little. Yet, what choice did I have? So, I turned to the man and smiled. "You've got yourself a deal."

"Great. Just a couple more things. Julian is standing in one of the hotel rooms across the street watching us. Don't look up there now. I don't want him to get any ideas. My recommendation would be for you to get yourself some lunch and then go up there and see him. And about lunch. Here's ten bucks. Treat yourself to something nice." He reached into his pocket, pulled up a folded piece of notebook paper, and handed it to me. "This is what Julian has been told about you. It would be best to keep that consistent."

The man walked away without another word. I took his money out of the bucket. Ten dollars. Better than almost any other day I'd had on the street. And that only meant one thing: Mickey D's for lunch. And no Dollar Menu. I was going to treat myself to a combo meal. Then I was going to find Julian Donahue and figure out what his story was.

*   *   *   *   *

I walked to the bathroom to get away from Julian and his fancy technology. Google. Psh. Who even knew what that was or how to use it? There's no way that thing was popular. He was probably playing a trick on me.

The bathroom disgusted me more than the "Two Girls, One Cup" video Julian conned me into *Googling.* Fucking prick. The sinks were coated in a solid inch of dust, none of the stalls had doors and some didn't even have walls, and brown stains covered the floor. I hoped they weren't shit, but deep down I knew the truth.

Overall, I'd say it was the perfect representation of the state of the public library system. I did my business and walked to the sink to wash my hands. Normally, I wouldn't bother, but it was necessary in that cesspool. The bathroom was the birthplace for all deadly infectious diseases; it was their ground zero. I wouldn't be surprised to learn that a new strain of the plague was brewing in there.

As I dried my hands with paper towels that were as smooth as sandpaper and as absorbent as notebook paper, someone spoke from behind me. I was so startled I nearly added my own streak to the floor.

"Having a little trouble?" the voice asked. It was male and sounded vaguely familiar, but I couldn't place it. He was right, though; I was struggling. I'd almost gone through one entire roll of paper towels, but my hands didn't seem to be getting any drier.

"Yeah," I said, "I think these paper towels might actually be making my hands wetter."

"I can't think of anything I care less about than the quality of the paper towels, Robert," the man said.

Admittedly, I was a bit caught off guard. I know Robert wasn't the most unique name, but so few people knew me by name. It couldn't be a coincidence. I hesitantly turned around, right arm cocked and at the ready. I truthfully had no idea what awaited me.

Well wouldn't you know, the man who asked me to betray Julian stood behind me. I never thought I'd be so relieved to see someone. "Jesus Christ, why are you sneaking up on me like that? And how the hell did you know we were here?"

"I know everything that you and Julian do." He said it as if it were as simple a fact as: $2 + 2 = 4$.

"So, what are you doing here?" I asked trying to hide the trepidation in my voice.

"I told you, it looks like you're having trouble. I'm here to guide you," the man who asked me to betray Julian said.

"Next question: what the hell does that mean?"

"If you could be a little more patient and kept your mouth shut for more than a second, I'd get to it." Gotta be honest: he was kind of a prick. Actually, more than kind of, but he did promise to get me off the streets, so I couldn't hold too much of a grudge. He started to dig through his pockets.

The man who asked me to betray Julian was now searching through pocket number three. The man who asked me to betray Julian. I didn't even know his name, and I doubted he'd tell me. He seemed like a man who valued his privacy, but still, it'd be nice to have something to call him.

"One more question: I know you probably won't tell me your real name, but do you have a nickname or something? I'm getting tired of calling you 'the man who asked me to betray Julian.'"

"You have no reason to be calling me anything. You have no business discussing me with anyone."

"That's true. And I haven't discussed you with anyone," I added, not wanting to upset him and lose my deal. "But what about when I think about you to myself?" That came out wrong. I quickly added, "for instance, when I turned around and saw you today, I thought, 'oh, it's just 'the man who asked me to betray Julian.'No reason to be concerned.' And that just sounds clunky."

He was beginning to lose his patience, but did his best to keep his composure. "I don't give a shit what you call me. Call me My Little Pony, for all I care."

I couldn't tell if My Little Pony was serious. And it didn't matter because that was absolutely not going to work. "That's not gonna work. We're gonna need to come up with something else."

He rubbed his forehead in frustration, though I don't think I was the sole cause. He was on pocket number seven now, after digging through all four pants pockets and both exterior suit pockets, now moving onto his left interior suit pocket. He had to be running low on pockets. "If you must call me something, call me...I don't know...Gray."

"Hold on one second." Gray looked at me, wondering what the fuck I was doing. "That'll work."

Gray looked angry, dumfounded, and annoyed, what I liked to call the *golden trifecta*. He reached into pocket number eight and found what he was searching for, a small, rectangular piece of paper. He handed it to me. "Try this."

I quickly read it. "What's this?"

"Just search it."

"You mean on Google? Do not get me started on Google. That stupid, fucking thing is so confusing. It makes no goddamn sense."

Gray's previous animosity turned to amusement. "I'm not sure there's ever been a simpler invention. If you're familiar with the process of how letters combine into words, you should be able to work it without a problem."

I looked down at the piece of paper and it stared back, trying to intimidate me. And it succeeded. "Nope. Can't do it. Can't be done."

"I don't have time for this," Gray said. "Just get out there and search that." He walked out without saying another word, which I thought was a little rude. Would a simple *goodbye* have killed him?

*   *   *   *   *

Yeah, you handle it, Julian. I'll just stand there and keep quiet because you're Mr. Smooth Talker. No one holds a candle to you when it comes to shooting the breeze with the high and mighty. Move over, Steve McQueen, there's a new King of Cool. You could sell Viagra to teenage boys and oil to the Gulf of Mexico and a bicycle to Stephen Hawking. *Of course* you can schmooze some rich guy with more money than he could ever spend.You do all the talking; I'll just stand silently at your side. That's *sure* to work. Arrogant prick.

While His Royal Smoothness continued to fumble over his words and hastily plan more hair-brained schemes, I took action, walking to the back of house. If I could just explain to Gorelli who I was and what we were doing here, surely he'd let us in.

I knocked on the sliding glass door, and Gorelli arrived with alarming quickness, almost like he was waiting for me. Even more surprisingly, he opened the door, something I never would have considered if I was in his situation.

"I hope you're planning to tell me what the hell you're really doing here."

"I'm working with Gray."

"Who the hell is Gray?"

At that moment, I realized my lack of knowledge of Gray was coming back to bite me in the ass. I knew next to nothing about the man. Hell, I didn't even know his real name. So, I did the best I could.

"Gray. I'm working with him to capture that guy that's out front. He's a shorter guy, nice suit."

"I have no idea who you're talking about. I don't know how you two managed to get in here, but I suggest you leave before I get security up here."

So, that didn't go the way I planned. For the life of me, I couldn't think of how next to proceed. Fortunately, I didn't have to ponder the thought too long because Gray appeared a moment later.

He did not address me, instead opting to go straight for the door. Rather than knocking like me, he barged right in.

"Carson, where are you?" Gray asked, sternly. He spoke with a quiet confidence that commanded the room. He was the type of person that you didn't want to keep waiting and he sure as fuck wasn't someone you wanted to defy. Gorelli swiftly appeared seconds later.

"What can I do for you, boss?" Gorelli asked. Then he looked past Gray and saw me. "You? What the fuck are you still doing here?"

Gray viscerally shook his head, but he did not lose his composure. In my few interactions with him, he'd had more than a few reasons to be upset, but he never lost his temper no matter how much contempt he felt.

"Do I only employ buffoons?" Gray asked. "On second thought, that's an insult to buffoons because even they could follow the superlatively simple tasks that I assign. Carson, I told you two people - a black guy and a white guy - were going to show up at your house today and it is imperative that you let them in. If my memory serves me, a black guy and a white guy showed up at your house not five minutes ago. So why the fuck are we standing back here like a bunch of dipshits with our thumbs up our asses? Is it because you want to orchestrate a circle jerk because I've got some backed up cum that's itching to get out? You just say the word, and I'll fall into formation."

Gorelli opened and closed his mouth several times, unable to form a coherent thought, and when he finally did, he spoke with the contrition of a three year old who'd just been caught taking a poop on the kitchen floor. "But...but they were dressed as package delivery workers. Look at him. How...how was I supposed to know?"

"B...b...b...because I don't pay you to be a fucking oblivious jackass." I have to admit, it felt good not be the one to feel the wrath of Gray for once. "And *you*," he turned to me. Maybe I spoke too soon. "Did it ever occur to you that maybe, just maybe, you should present yourself as a respectable human being instead of looking like another commoner."

Both Gorelli and I were dumfounded.

"Now get the fuck back inside and try to make me forget that I ever had to be here today."

Chapter 37

Doonsbury closed the diary.

"I helped Robert in those situations and at the gas station when you couldn't find Bellvavick's address." I knew Robert couldn't have done that himself. "I've been watching from afar, interjecting when needed, but mostly I've been watching with enjoyment the situations you two have gotten yourself in. God, you two have done have done some stupid shit. I must admit, it's been quite entertaining. When you couldn't figure out the logo! That had to be one of the funniest things I have ever seen! It took everything in my power not to drop in and give you another hint, but it was so satisfying to sit and watch you struggle. But you did it! You solved the mystery and made it here. And now you're all alone. No one's on your side. Not even Robert. And do you know why? Because Robert was never yours. He was always mine. I thought a smart guy like you might have picked up on that by now. No matter where you were, no matter what you were doing, I was always one step ahead pulling the strings. I got to Robert before you did. I was able to convince him that I had a lot more to offer him than you. Earlier, I asked why you didn't want to kill him, but I knew the answer to that because I know you, Julian. I knew you never had any intention to kill him. And I knew you would do everything in your power to find me. Of course, that was an impossible mission without a little help. You see, I wanted you to find me, Julian. From the start, you were my target. Now that I have you here, it's time to have a little fun."

Chapter 38

On cue, Robert burst back into the room, gun drawn and pointed at me. I can't say I was too surprised by his betrayal. My gut always told me not to trust the man, but I knew I needed his help. I should have known from the moment that I met him that he was someone that I shouldn't have put my faith in. And if not then, it should have been abundantly clear when I watched how ruthlessly he tortured the fake Bellavick and how apathetic he was when he murdered the homeless man. I guess I'd been hoping that I might be able to convince him that I wasn't his enemy, that I was his only hope. Alas, I was unable to prevail, and somewhere, deep down, I always knew that was going to be the result. Fuck him. He was a douchebag anyway. I wouldn't wish his presence upon the Devil. I had to admit, things didn't look good for me, but if I did die, I would at least have solace in the fact that I would never have to see his face or hear his voice again.

"So, I guess I won't get to defend my title at the golf tournament this weekend," I said. The writing was on the wall. There was no way I was going to walk out of this alive, but I wasn't going to let these two win. I wasn't going to crack and I sure as hell wasn't going to beg for my life. They weren't going to get that satisfaction. If this was it for me, then I was going down swinging.

"I'm afraid I don't see what you mean," Doonsbury said, his face contorted in a look of confusion and perhaps...disappointment, try as he might to hide it. That was exactly what I wanted. I was winning. Besides that whole imminent death thing.

"I'm not stupid. I know my fate. If you're going to kill me, just do it now. I'm not going to suck your dick to cling to a few more minutes, if that's what you had in mind." I cracked a huge grin, leaned back in my chair, and kicked my feet up on Doonsbury's desk. That oughta piss him off.

Doonsbury sat quietly for moment. When he finally moved, he matched my grin with one of his own. The words that followed were calm, but his stare showed just how badly he wanted me dead. "Oh, I do intend to kill you, you can be sure of that. But I like to play with my food before I eat it."

"Are you saying you're a cannibal?" I quipped.

Nothing happened for almost a minute. Then, Doonsbury stared daggers at Robert, but he was too busy looking out the window to notice. Finally, Robert turned back, but his expression was blank when he met Doonsbury's eyes. Doonsbury moved his eyes between me and Robert several times, but Robert shrugged. So, Doonsbury nodded at me and then at the door to the conference room. Robert just shook his head.

"Just take him to the fucking conference room."

Robert walked over and leaned in to grab me, but I stood up out of the chair and backed away before he had a chance. "Touch me and I will have you on your knees begging for your life faster than you can find a reason to bitch about rich people."

It had to be the most pathetic surrender in recorded human history. I was being taken at gunpoint by a homeless man. Then, I was going to be held captive by a maniacal CEO, only to endure whatever twisted form of torture he saw fit. Most people in my situation would put up a bit more of a fight and would probably have to be forcibly dragged to their prison, but I thought my lethargy and utter indifference would only fuel Doonsbury's fury.

Robert ushered me to the conference room, then left without saying a word, closing the door behind him. I didn't bother to check if the door was locked; it probably was, but even if it wasn't, I hardly stood a chance to escape past

Doonsbury and Robert, let alone make it out of the building unscathed.

The conference room was the pinnacle of decadence. A magnificent wooden table rested in the middle of the room, which looked to be an exact replica of the table in the Cabinet Room. It was surrounded by what would have been the most plush leather chairs I'd ever seen, had I not just seen the chair at Doonsbury's desk. State of the art technology filled the room. A small projector hung from the ceiling, but I got the feeling it was one of those 'it's not the size of the boat' things. A massive screen stood across from it, covering the entirety of the far wall. A group of technological instruments sat on shelves in the corner. I couldn't distinguish any of it, but I could tell they were highly sophisticated. Trevor would have had an orgasm just from looking at the devices. All that and I doubted Doonsbury ever held an official meeting in the room.

It didn't take long for boredom to set in. My phone only had fifty percent battery left, and the way smartphones are designed, I'd be lucky if it lasted two more hours. Since I didn't know how long Doonsbury planned to "play" with me before killing me, I needed to ration my battery life out for as long as possible. I allowed myself fifteen minutes of phone time. By my sixteenth minute in the room, I was going insane. If Doonsbury didn't kill me soon, I was sure to defy science and die of boredom. No one stopped in the room for the rest of the night and a few hours later (it could have been days, since time had slowed to a lethargic crawl) the lights in Doonsbury's office shut off. I curled up on the table, made myself as comfortable as possible, and tried to sleep.

I awoke the next morning, still in the conference room. That meant I hadn't died in my sleep. I have to admit, I was a little disappointed. That would have made things a lot easier for me.

My newfound free time gave me ample opportunity to think. I reflected on my life and the decisions I made that brought me here. That instantly improved my mood. There were a lot of great memories to look back upon. The month I spent in Argentina doing nothing but exploring the land, drinking on the beach, and having sex with beautiful women. Dinner at the White House when I got to meet the President. And have sex with his twin daughters. The time I got pulled on stage to sing "Daughter" with Pearl Jam. They even told a group of girls that I was part of the band, which led to my first and only foursome. Basically, my life boiled down to a series of wild, crazy, unforgettable experiences culminating in sex. Lots and lots and lots of sex. But despite all the awesomeness that was my life, I could not get one thought out of head. I'd accepted the fact that Doonsbury wanted to kill me, but I didn't have the faintest hint as to why. Why was he so hell-bent on torturing me? Why did he lead me on the wild goose chase to find him? What had I done that made him so inclined to psychologically torment me? If I was going to die, I at least deserved to know why.

Some time later, Robert walked in. Judging by the position of the sun in the sky, I guessed it was around noon. He set a tray of food and drink on the table and left the room, neither of us breaking the silence. I took a sip out of the bottle of water and examined the food. It turned out to be an *immensely* nutritious and substantive cheese sandwich. My favorite. Eleven seconds later, the sandwich was gone, and I swear it only made me hungrier. I only took a few more sips out of my water. I didn't know if or when I was going to be replenished, so I needed to make sure it lasted.

It turned out to be for naught, however, as Robert returned before the sun set. He dropped another tray off and immediately left again. This continued for two more days, Robert bringing me sandwiches and water, then leaving in silence. No mention of Doonsbury or his master plan to torture me. I never even saw my captor or heard his voice in the other room. By the third day, I'd had enough. I had to do something.

The next time Robert set the tray down on the table and turned his back to leave, I tackled him from behind. I patted my hands on his hips, torso, and legs to see if he was still carrying the gun. I couldn't find one on him, not that I was surprised. Doonsbury would have been unwise to allow him to continue to carry the weapon, just in case he ever decided to bite the hand that fed him. Unfortunately, my search caused me to lose the element of surprise. Before I could react, Robert flipped me on my back and climbed on top of me. This was the first time I could remember being disappointed by being mounted. Robert punched me in the face. Then again. He was much larger and stronger than me, so I knew I wasn't going to be able to overpower him. I was going to have to outsmart him, which hardly seemed like a daunting task. When Robert threw his next punch, I intercepted it and used his momentum to throw him off me. I seized the opportunity to gain the upper hand, jumping on top of Robert and delivering several blows of my own. Robert used his superior strength to roll me off him. We wrestled on the ground for several minutes, exchanging fisticuffs. As we rolled on the floor, we knocked over two chairs and slammed into the wall a handful of times. The ruckus must have caused quite a commotion because Doonsbury stormed into the room and his face was livid.

"What the hell is going on in here?" Doonsbury marched over and tried to pull us apart. He struggled to lift Robert's weight, but eventually the homeless man relented and stood up of his own volition.

"Get the fuck out of here," Doonsbury said, shoving Robert toward the door.

Doonsbury slowly strolled toward me, eyeing me the entire time. He stopped a few feet in front of me, but continued to stare. I was still laying on the ground, having not gotten up since Doonsbury tried to pull Robert off me. I was beginning to feel a little awkward about my positioning, but I could tell Doonsbury felt the same awkwardness, so I was determined to hold my ground.

"I see boredom has finally bested you. You're going to regret the moment that happened." Doonsbury exited the room. He must have been spending too much time with Robert because he was starting to absorb some of the homeless man's cryptic ramblings.

As I turned over to climb to my feet, I noticed something out of the corner of my eye, something that hadn't been there when I first entered the room. It was a small black notebook, and when I got closer to pick it up, I realized it was Robert's journal. I fought the urge to open it and sift through its contents. The last thing I needed was for Robert to walk in and see me pouring through his most intimate secrets. I stashed the journal behind one of the doohickeys (you know, the technical term) in the corner, vowing to return to it later.

Over the next few days, I would come to regret ever wondering what Doonsbury had in store for me. It started out innocently enough. I'd been sitting in silence for several hours, waiting for Doonsbury to do his worst, when I heard the faint sound of music. At first, I assumed my newfound arch-nemesis was trying to unwind by listening to some tunes, but then the music grew louder, and it occurred to me that the sound came from inside the meeting room. The first few notes were an upbeat violin melody. It was catchy, but something about it bothered me. Then the lyrics came in. "I used to rule the world," Chris Martin, the antichrist himself, sang, and I died a little inside. I counted down every second the horrible drebb played, and by the good graces of God, the song ended exactly four minutes and one second later. I breathed a sigh of relief when the two-hundred-forty-one seconds that seemed to last for two-hundred-forty-one days ended. I should have known better than to let my guard down; just when I thought it was all over, "Paradise" started to play. If I could have found a rusty nail, I would have punctured my ears drums.

And so it continued, one Coldplay song after another, like the Devil forgot to press shuffle on the playlist Hitler and Mussolini created for him. If only there were a chalkboard I could scratch my nails on or solid metal I could grind against asphalt to drown out the sounds. Every beat of the drum, every strum of the guitar, every word out of the singer's mouth was like having chunks of my skin clawed off. The pain was slow, agonizing, and persistent. At every decrescendo I prayed to every God, prophet, sacred animal, and pseudo-religious figure I could think of to end my suffering, whether it be stopping the music or ending my life. At that point, I honestly didn't care. Actually, I preferred the latter, because if I continued to live, then I'd have to go on with the memory of this day. I tried plugging my ears, but every time I did, the volume increased exponentially, rendering my finger plugs useless. I contemplated banging my head on the floor. At least if I was unconscious Chris Martin's voice would cease to terrorize me. But I'm not sure the benefits outweighed the risks.

The longer the music played, the more the sound reverberated off the walls, the deeper it penetrated my soul, until I thought I would never be able to hear anything but Coldplay music again, even if my prayers were answered and it stopped. I thought my entire body was going to erupt, vital organs splattering the walls. I flipped the table over. I wanted to throw it against the wall, but it was significantly heavier than I estimated. I tried to do the same with one of the chairs, but it proved equally stifling, so I rolled it as hard as I could against one of the walls. Apparently, that was the magic answer because the music stopped a few seconds later.

I thought that would be the end of it for me, but, try as I might, I couldn't get the obnoxious noise out of my head. I tried making random noises, I tried singing songs that didn't make me feel like my insides had been lit by a flamethrower, but none of it worked. I rolled around on the ground, covering my ears until I tired myself out. When I finally did, I crawled to the corner and laid in the fetal position, waiting for sleep to fall upon me. But it never came.

Chapter 39

When I'd accepted that I was not going to be able to sleep, I racked my brain for ways to distract myself. My phone was dead, so that was out. At a lack for better options, I decided to look through Robert's journal. Though they may be the nonsensical ramblings of a madman, at least they might allow my mind to wander for a few minutes.

As expected, the journal was so monotonous that I almost fell asleep reading the first page. Though sleep would have been a much more suitable alternative, something told me to continue reading. His entries were intricately detailed. It looked as though he'd chronicled every significant moment from the last ten years, if not longer. Even the biggest nerds in my high school who I used to torment with wedgies, noogies, and swirlies didn't take notes this detailed.

The journal did, however, confirm Doonsbury's assertion that he'd been working with Robert the whole time, even before I met the man. There were entries about each of their meetings, each of which was precisely written word-for-word as Doosbury read it.

As I continued to read, I found one very curious entry, an entry about Clay, whom Robert killed several days earlier. He explained that the reason he killed Clay was because the junkie had somehow played a role in Robert's demise or was responsible for his continued homelessness. Oddly enough, it was one of the few areas that Robert didn't go into excruciating detail.

I continued to read until I came to the most recent entry. It was short, but got its point across nonetheless. *Synapse: kill word; when ~~Gray~~ Doonsbury says this, kill Julian.* Of course Doonsbury wasn't bluffing. He was going to have me killed, and Robert was going to do it.

Chapter 40

I was so immersed in Robert's journal that I jumped off the ground at the sound of a loud crackle of static. I turned my head, realizing that the noise originated from the projector on the wall across from me. It took a few minutes before it dawned on me just how loud the noise was. The sound filled the room; I doubted whether I'd be able to hear anything from Dounsbury's office. The roar was deafening. As annoying as it was, the static was infinitely more pleasant than Coldplay. Great. Just when I got their atrocious drebb out of my head, they burrow back into my brain like a termite, which sounded like an excellent alternative.

Suddenly the static cut into the feed of an empty room. It reminded me of a police interrogation room. A steel table and single steel chair sat in the center of the room. Aside from those two objects, the room was empty. Still, I found myself unable to peel my eyes away from the screen. With nothing but The Band Who Must Not Be Named to entertain me (I could not stress just how bored I was that I referred to the previous night's torture as "entertainment") for almost five days, I would have jumped at the chance to watch an ant crawl across the room, which made the empty room as appealing to me as reality television is to the average, brainwashed American.

After twenty minutes of non-stop, jaw-dropping, sit-on-the-edge-of-your-seat fun, the door opened. A person wearing a dark, baggy shirt and gray sweatpants with a bag over his or her head was led into the room by none other than my old friend, Dale Showen. He sat the figure down and removed the bag. My heart sank as he urged the figure to look at the camera; it was my sister. She couldn't keep the tears from streaming down her face. The look on her face was a mixture of terror and longing. She needed someone to save her. For her entire life, I'd always been there to protect her, and it tore me apart knowing that I could do nothing for her.

Showen walked in front of her, turning his back to me. He pulled a handheld device out of his pocket that I didn't recognize. It was about the size of a smartphone, but it was matte gray and the only thing on it was a green, circular button. Whatever it was, it couldn't be good.

Showen turned toward the camera, an evil grin spreading across his face. A tear rolled down my cheek. Showen pressed the button and my sister's body convulsed and she let out a blood curdling scream, an electric current passing through her body. He waited a few seconds, and then pressed the button again, the results being the same. I closed my eyes and turned away after that, but Doonsbury's voice filled the room.

"Don't look away now, Julian. It'll only get worse."

Worse? How could it get any worse? Though I doubted he had prepared a more severe form of punishment, I wasn't willing to call his bluff. I turned back to the screen and watched as Showen continued to shock my sister for the better part of the next thirty minutes. With each wave of electricity, her screams became more feeble. Her head dipped; she seemed too exhausted to control her body. As bad as listening to Coldplay on a continuous loop had been last night, this was infinitely worse. I would have done anything to trade places with her, to take her pain away.

When Showen stopped the atrocity, he approached my sister, feeling her neck for a pulse. Then he addressed the camera.

"Don't worry, Julian. She's still alive...for now." He pulled something from his side, but his body obstructed the view. He raised the object to her temple and I realized it was some sort of blunt object.

"No!" I yelled. "Please! Please don't! I'll do anything. Kill me instead!"

As if he could hear, Showen turned toward the camera, his smile even more maniacal than before. He wound up and let loose a swing that would have made Barry Bonds proud.

I lost all control as I saw her lifeless body crumple to the ground, blood spewing everywhere. I grabbed one of the chairs, anger and adrenaline fueling my strength, and threw it at the window. I expected the object to easily break through the glass, but it simply ricocheted off. Fucking bulletproof glass.

My fury didn't subside at my inability to send the chair plummeting one hundred stories. I threw the rack of electronic devices at the far wall. I flipped the table over so that it was upended on its other side. I banged on the door, punching it, kicking it, ramming my shoulder into it. The only thing that stopped me was a loud cackling.

I turned back to the screen to see Showen howling in laughter. My sister was now upright in the chair. She looked a little worse for the wear, but she was alive.

"Don't you know not to believe everything you see on TV?" the former surgeon squawked.

Over the next few hours, Showen inflicted various forms of torture upon my sister. Frank Davacchio and Carson Gorelli made cameos in some of the acts as well. The three men laid my sister on the table slowly dripped water onto her forehead. Chinese Water Torture. I assumed that would be ineffective. I mean, it's just a few drops of water; how bad could it really be? But it proved to be even more excruciating than the electric shocks. They also flogged her with handheld switches and used a plastic bag to suffocate her, only relenting when she was on the verge of passing out, letting her catch her breath for no more than ten seconds before returning to the act. Each method was punctuated with a mock execution: decapitation (how they managed to fake that, I have no idea), a knife violently thrust into her cranium, and, finally, four gunshots to the head.

Throughout the torture and 'executions' I protested, yelled, screamed, and threw everything I could get my hands on. Each time, Doonsbury warned me to calm down if I didn't want her to suffer even more gravely. I knew the scenes were falsified to torment me, but they were conducted with such an incredible amount of realism that it was nearly impossible not to take seriously. Plus, those four psychopaths were so unstable that they'd be willing to actually execute her, but only after getting every visceral reaction they could out of me.

After Doonsbury's cronies picked my sister back up off the floor yet again, the video feed shut off. Still, I couldn't pull my eyes away from the screen.

"Boy, you've really done a number in here." I didn't even react. I'd had enough of his taunts. "It's rude not to look someone in the eyes when they talk to you, you know?"

I turned, stunned to see Doonsbury standing in the doorway.

"Still haven't figured it out yet, have you?" Doonsbury asked. "I really thought all the Coldplay would give it away. And when that wasn't enough, I thought the executions would be a dead giveaway. Maybe I overestimated your intelligence."

I was puzzled. I didn't know if the lack of sleep and mental exhaustion he'd put me through the last couple days had completely fried my brain's ability to process information or if he intentionally spoke cryptically to piss me off. "I don't know what the fuck you're talking about." Whatever it was, I didn't have the patience for any more of his fucking games. I was going to end this one way or another.

"Surely you must be wondering why I'd be willing to go through all this trouble for you, Julian. Why it's so important for me to torment you and eventually see to your demise. Don't you want to know who I am or how I know you? Come on, Julian. Just take a shot in the dark."

Realization hit me like an anvil on the Wile E. Coyote. But how could it possibly be? "I hope you didn't have that dick when I first met you."

328

Chapter 41

The following is the demented explanation Doonsbury gave for my suffering.

*   *   *   *   *

After months of painstaking research, our hard work had finally come to fruition. We were finally going to present our proposal and forever change the landscape of neurology. And I was going to be leading the presentation! It was the biggest moment of my career. I'd been practicing nonstop for more than a week, making sure every word of the presentation was perfect. I painstakingly poured through my notes, all my research, and had coworkers ask mock questions to ready myself for anything the board could throw at me.

Dr. Tindall accompanied me to the conference room where we would meet the Board of Directors. I tried to object to his presence - I could give the presentation just fine on my own, thank you very much - but he insisted. I was in no position to argue with him. Dr. Tindall was the leader of the team, after all, and he exhibited considerable sway over the board. He could have halted the presentation if he desired as much, so it was best to jump through all his little hoops and play the game his way, even if his insistence on standing at my side made me feel like I was being babysat.

The board was already waiting in the conference room when Dr. Tindall and I arrived. They were seven of the most snotty, stuck up, egotistical men I'd ever meant. And why were they all men? Of course, that question is rhetorical. I know the answer. Despite the fact that there were surely many qualified women to join the board, these chauvinistic assholes would never let a woman into their boys' club. It was despicable.

I won't bore you with the details, but the presentation went better than I ever could have imagined. I perfectly outlined our groundbreaking discoveries and how this new information could completely change the way we study the brain and treat brain injuries and diseases. If our research proved correct, we may even be able to find ways to reverse or even cure the effects of Alzheimer's, Huntington's Disease, and memory loss. My presentation was, objectively, compelling, and even the board did not raise questions as I spoke.

When I finished, however, they did have a few queries.

"Dr. Tindall," one of the board members whose name escapes me, began, "what makes this research so much more impactful than the research that is already being done on Alzheimer's, Huntington's Disease, and other brain diseases?" I don't know why he didn't ask me that. It was my presentation.

Dr. Tindall's answer was essentially the same as what mine would have been. "While the research my team has conducted may not be fundamentally different than what is currently being done, we believe we have identified several key factors and causes for these diseases that previously have not been discovered. We have also refuted several claims made by some of the top scientists in these fields that prove some or even all of the effects of these diseases are not irreversible."

"Dr. Tindall, who has been chiefly responsible for these newfound discoveries?" Again, why didn't they ask me? It was *my* presentation and *my* research.

"Samantha has played an integral role in the new discoveries that have come to light, but this has really been a team effort. We would not be where we are today without every member of our team." I hated that he called me Samantha and not Dr. Salin. It was such a sign of disrespect. Almost as disrespectful as not admitting that this entire presentation was based on my research. Everyone else on the team, even Dr. Tindall, believed I was wasting my time at first. But I proved them all wrong.

"Dr. Tindall, do you wholeheartedly believe in this research and stand by the information that was presented today?" Now I was really getting pissed off. I'd just proven to them how valuable this research could be. If this was a court of law, I would have proven beyond a reasonable doubt that this research was crucial and groundbreaking. The jury wouldn't have even needed to deliberate.

"I do. If you grant us the means to further pursue this research through expanded experiments and improved equipment, then I truly believe we can slow the effects of these horrible diseases and maybe one day cure them."

That was the final question the board members had. I thought it to be very unsubstantive and lacking depth, but I was not going to put up a fight. I knew better than that. I packed up my materials and headed for the door. As expected, Dr. Tindall stayed behind to chit-chat with the board members. As the door closed, I heard one of the board members say:

"Now that we've given Samantha her little moment in the spotlight, maybe her tampon won't be so tightly wedged in her vagina. Let's head to lunch, then you can give us the real presentation after, Dr. Tindall."

*   *   *   *   *

Doonsbury directly addressed me.

"After that, I had you take care of him. Or so I thought."

Now, back to our regularly scheduled lunatic history lesson.

*   *   *   *   *

Now that Robert was out of the way (yes, I'd stopped calling him Dr. Tindall - that change came about the second he ceased to be my colleague) and every shred of his existence had been scrubbed, maybe I'd get the respect I deserved. He'd never seen me as a peer, but rather as a worker bee who served no other purpose than to get my hands dirty and make him look good. My other colleagues, on the other hand, had always recognized my contributions and were grateful for my dedication and impact. Or so I thought.

When I got to the new lab, it looked like a tornado had ripped through the place, causing chaos wherever it touched. Beakers were overturned, liquids of all colors flowed across the various tables, and the microscopes were so dirty that they were covered in more germs and matter than the samples they were used to study. It was absolutely disgusting, and I was going to be the one who had to clean it all up because the team treated me like their mother, all because I was the only woman. I swear, I spent more time cleaning the lab than I did actually conducting research or experiments. But this was it for me. It was going to stop now. One way or another.

"Would it kill you guys to clean up after yourselves just one time? Or are you just waiting for the maid to do it again?"

Either they were too absorbed in their work to hear me or they'd blatantly chosen to ignore me. My bet was on the latter. I was not having it.

"Clean this shit up right this instant!" I exclaimed. At five foot seven, I did not command the room, per se, but the old adage 'hell hath no fury like a woman scorned' persisted. The three men actually began to clean up the mess. If I had to be a bitch once in a while to get things done, then so be it.

A few minutes later, one of the board members stopped by to check on our progress. They'd started to come to the lab at such annoyingly frequent intervals that I was going to have to tell them off if the pace didn't slow soon.

"Looks like you're getting a lot done," he sarcastically said. Bite your tongue, Samantha. Bite your tongue.

"We were just finishing up one of our most important experiments, actually," one of my colleagues, Dr. Frostwick said, "but Samantha stormed in here and demanded that we clean." He turned to the board member and pointed to his genitals and crudely enacted what was supposed to be a vagina bleeding. My blood boiled.

"Well, it's good to see that at least some of you have your priorities straight. We know who the real contributors are, and I can assure you that your contributions do not go unrecognized."

That was it. It was time to do something about the lack of respect. I walked to my desk and tried to keep my composure as I plotted my revenge.

I was the last one in the lab that day, just as I'd planned. When my colleagues went home for the day, I walked over to the most frequently used outlet in the room and removed the cover. I'd earned a second degree in electrical engineering when I was in undergrad. Though I had no intention to use the degree, I saw it as an added challenge. I never thought it would actually come in handy.

I tinkered with several of the wires until I was content with my work. I popped the cover back on and screwed it back into place. The adjustments were unnoticeable. They would have no idea what hit them. As soon as something was plugged into the outlet, it would send an electrical charge so powerful that the whole place would explode. That, coupled with the abundance of flammable items in the lab, would destroy the place in a matter of minutes.

It did not take long for news of the explosion to spread. It was on every news channel that night. I could not help myself from smiling as the anchors speculated causes for the disaster and read obituaries of the deceased scientists. Though Samantha Salin had not physically been involved in the explosion, she might as well have been. She died the day she failed to seduce an arrogant pretty boy, the first time her femininity had let her down. She was never coming back. It was time to make a change, to become someone that would not only be respected, but adored.

Chapter 42

I was stunned when Doonsbury/Salin finished his (her?) tale, and only half of that was because I was unsure what name and pronoun to use. I made a mental note to stick with Doonsbury and male pronouns, as that was what I'd used most commonly. I don't know how the transgender community preferred these situations to be handled, and frankly I didn't care, least of all for Doonsbury.

Anyway, back to the main point. I was completely awestruck when *Doonsbury* finished *his* tale. For a moment, I wished I was the guy from *Click* so that I had a remote that could control the world because I desperately needed to pause for a while to reflect and process all the information I just received. First of all, Doonsbury had once been Samantha Salin, an extremely hot woman who was also a scientist. Doonsbury was the person who hired me to kill Robert all those years ago, the person who forever altered the course of my life. More importantly, though, was the fact that Robert had once been a scientist as well. Though his tale of once being a prominent businessman was a fabricated lie, it was true that he'd once had a bright future ahead of him. Despite the droll stories stories he told and general annoyingness, he was so much sharper than any other homeless person I'd ever come across. If he'd once been a scientist - and a good one from the indication Doonsbury's story gave me - that meant he really did have the intelligence to weigh Doonsbury's offer, accept it, and lead me around this whole time. Every move he'd made had been calculated. Every word he spoke, every story he told, carefully crafted to draw me in to trust him.

"Imagine my disappointment," Doonsbury continued, "when you didn't come back that night. You told me you would return when you finished the job. You said you would fuck me like I'd never been fucked before."

I couldn't let Doonsbury continue without interjecting. "If this is all some big ploy just to get me to fuck you, then I hate to disappoint you again, but I'd sooner turn the gun on myself than put my penis within five feet of you. I'm worried that just thinking about it will make me flaccid for the rest of my life."

Was this really the time for Doonsbury to talk about me not fucking him? Was this all really because I hadn't given him my special 'Julian Lovin'? And now I'm really regretting my decision to use masculine pronouns because the last thing I wanted to do was picture myself fucking another man. I made a mental note to switch back to female pronouns if the conversation on sex continued.

"Jesus Christ, Julian, how fucking dim are you? Is sex the only thing you think about?" I thought about intervening to answer in the affirmative, but I didn't see that helping me in any way. "The only reason I bring that up is because I knew that when you didn't return to fuck me that something had gone wrong, that you never did finish the job. Because there's nothing - or more accurately *almost* nothing - that would stop you from having sex. So I went to investigate, and by the time I got to the scene, I saw Robert being loaded into an ambulance. I don't how I knew it, but I knew right then that he was going to survive. You failed me, Julian. And now you must pay the price."

Chapter 43

Doonsbury summoned Robert to join us in the room. He was stone faced as he approached Doonsbury and me, sitting on opposite sides of the desk. He remained standing as he waited for his next direction.

"Robert, your gun is in the safe next door. Go get it." Doonsbury tossed him the keys.

So, this is it. This is where it all ends. Truthfully, I wasn't scared of dying. I know that sounds like I'm trying to be a tough guy, but it wasn't that at all. The only thing on my mind was my sister. What was going to happen to her? I had to hope that my death would bring about her release and return to safety. If that happened, then I could die with no regrets. Except for the blackjack dealer at Mandalay Bay. I was still kicking myself for not sealing the deal with her. If that was my only real regret, then I'd lived a pretty damn good life.

As we waited for Robert to return with his gun, Frank Davacchio, Dale Showen, and Carson Gorelli joined us in Doonsbury's office.

"Oh, goodie. A reunion!" I mockingly exclaimed.

Robert returned less than two minutes later. Of all the times for him to show some competence, it had to be now. Doonsbury wasted no time in giving the kill order. "Synapse."

I braced myself for my impending doom, but it didn't come. I turned around to see Robert standing dumbfounded. I'm not even sure he knew that Doonsbury spoke to him. I really shouldn't have overestimated his competence.

"Synapse," Doonsbury repeated.

Once again, Robert didn't react. What the hell was going on? Was he choosing this time to take a stand against Doonsbury? If so, I wasn't going to argue with him.

"Damn it, Robert. Synapse! That means you're supposed to kill him."

Robert's expression was like a deer in headlights. It felt like I'd been hit by a ton of bricks. I finally understood what happened to Robert.

"Can I at least say something before I die?" I interjected.

"I guess so," Doonsbury said, "but make it quick. I have a tee time in thirty minutes."

"But today's the day of the tournament."

"I know. I heard there was going to be an opening, so I pulled some strings and got myself a spot."

That motherfucker. Still, I couldn't worry about that. I had another, slightly bigger, issue to address. I turned to Robert as I spoke.

"You don't remember anything, do you? There's no point pretending; I read your journal. You have no idea what happened to you, no idea why you're really homeless. That's why you were in the abandoned building, wasn't it? You were trying to figure it out. You've been trying to figure it out this whole time."

Robert's grip on the gun tightened, but he didn't shoot. He was genuinely interested in what I had to say.

"Lucky for you, I know what happened to you sixteen years ago."

I chanced a glance at Doonsbury. He didn't seem concerned by what I was about to say. Maybe he thought he was calling a bluff, that I hadn't really put all the pieces together. Or maybe he thought the truth was so absurd that Robert would never believe it. Or maybe he thought Robert would kill me anyway. Whatever the reason, I knew it was a mistake on his part to let me keep talking.

"Sixteen years ago, when you were on your way home from work, I shot you."

I really took a risk revealing that so candidly without any of the back story. Robert raised the gun and aimed it at my head, but he still did not pull the trigger. Despite the severe head wound, he was still intelligent enough to know that there was still more to my story.

"I know that the story you told me about your life wasn't true, but parts of it were. The bullet wounds must have caused some trauma to your head and memory loss. That's why you weren't ever able to return to work at the same capacity. That's the real reason why you've been homeless all these years."

It was hard to get a read on Robert. His intense look seemed to have lessened. I presumed he was having a hard time processing the information. He'd been searching for answers for the better part of the last sixteen years. He killed Clay because he knew that the fellow homeless man (I don't care that he had a car, he was still homeless in my book) had played some role in ruining his life. Now, after all this time, he finally had a concrete explanation. Sure, he wouldn't remember the next day unless he wrote it down, but I still couldn't even begin to imagine how having some semblance of an answer made him feel.

"When I saw what I'd done to you, I felt horrible. There was so much blood. That night scarred me. That's the reason I haven't owned a gun in sixteen years, why I was so adamantly against you getting the gun you're holding right now. That's why I don't actually kill any of the people that I'm hired to kill. If I could take it all back, I would." I paused for a moment. "Don't go getting any ideas. It's not because I've grown to like you or anything like that. I still think you're an unbearable prick. I just couldn't believe I'd done that to another human. I could hardly live with myself after that night."

A quick piece of advice: if someone is holding your life in their hands, it's probably best not to insult them. But I didn't want Robert to think I was begging for my life, that I was only revealing this information in a desperate hope that he might spare my life. I'd already accepted my fate. I was a dead man. But I had an agenda.

"There's one more thing." I quickly glanced at Doonsbury again. He looked to be almost as interested in my story as Robert. Was he an idiot? If he'd had any intelligence whatsoever, he would have silenced me that second.

"I didn't choose to kill you at random. I was hired. You were a target. A beautiful woman named Samantha Salin paid me $25,000 to kill you." I could tell the name sounded familiar to Robert, but he couldn't quite place it. "I believe she was a colleague of yours back when you were a scientist. She was always jealous of you, jealous that you got all the attention for what she thought was her work. She thought the scientific community was sexist, that a woman couldn't possibly be responsible for such groundbreaking research.

Surely, her male team lead must be responsible. She thought that with you out of the picture, she would get the credit she deserved and the spotlight would finally be on her. But she was wrong. The scientific community still refused to recognize her accomplishments, so she did the only thing she could think of turn the tides in her favor. She had a sex change and used the research you two did to build a massive company. And she's in this room. Michael Doonsbury is really Samantha Salin. He's the one who hired me to kill you sixteen years ago."

Shit was going to hit the fan. And believe me, it did. If this was a rap battle, that would have been a pretty epic mic drop.

Doonsbury and his pions lost their fucking minds at the accusation. I'm not sure Davacchio, Showen, or Gorelli knew Doonsbury's true identity. Judging by the looks of confusion and hushed conversation, I'd say they didn't. In the ensuing chaos, one of the men cut out all power to the floor. The office was pitch black. Out of the darkness, I head Doonsbury's voice. He'd finally decided to speak up. Too bad for him, it was already too late.

"You're really going to believe that story, Robert? He's just saying that so that you won't kill him. Don't be a fool. You know that Julian is not a trustworthy man. He'd say anything to get people to bend to his wishes. You must see through the deception and lies. I can give you a place to live and food to eat. I can give you a new life. All you have to do is kill him."

I chuckled. "That's where you're wrong. I'm not saying any of this to try to save my life. I already know I'm a goner. Robert, I know you're going to kill me. And I really don't blame you after what I did. But if I am going to die, at least let me watch that bitch die first."

Without waiting for another word, Robert fired four shots in the dark.

Chapter 44

We walked down the hallway of the local hospital, my sister and I. The hospital was probably number three on my list of places-I-never-want-to-visit. Having already visited the first two (the public library and bus line, respectively) in the past two weeks, I can't say I was overly excited to make a journey to number three. The whole place reeked of death and old people, an odor combination I wouldn't have wished on my worst enemy. Scratch that. I would have wished it on Doonsbury, but he was dead now. None of that mattered anymore. I was with my sister again. She'd escaped (mostly) unscathed. It still felt surreal.

I still don't know why Robert spared my life. I'd stopped trying to understand him or his actions a long time ago. He was even more of an enigma than I first thought. Still, I was grateful for his mercy. Just don't tell him I said that.

It took quite a bit of finessing and persuasion to get us out of legal trouble. After all, we had just killed the CEO and the three most powerful executives of the largest neurological company in the world. Well, technically, Robert killed them, but I was viewed as his accomplice. The police may not care about the death of a homeless man or a junky, but they had a *few* questions to ask about the deaths of those four. I spent almost four hours in police interrogation telling them the whole story (minus the whole hired to kill Robert thing - but they didn't *need* to know that). When it was all said and done, I managed to convince them of our innocence, that we acted in self-defense. We were absolved of all blame. And Robert thought he was the smooth talker.

Apparently, Vindicta Neuroscience and Technology had developed a device that could reverse the effects of memory loss caused by brain trauma. If it worked like it was supposed to, it could heal the brain, allowing the user's memories to return and returning the neurological pathways back to their original state. Robert discovered it in the side room when he went to retrieve his gun. After shooting Doonsbury and his minions, Robert and I found my sister on one of the lower floors. The meeting was tearful, and my sister and I were emotional, too. After some introductions, Robert rushed back to the side room with the machine.

Unfortunately for him, he didn't understand the intricacies of the machine and passed out after using it. Hence why I was in the hospital. Actually, that wasn't really the reason. I was perfectly content letting him recover on his own and never seeing him again, but my sister insisted we pay the man a visit. I was seriously contemplating whether I'd made the right decision by deciding to try to rescue her.

As we approached the bed, Robert opened his eyes.

"How are you feeling?" my sister asked, gently stroking his arm.

"My head is killing me."

"Of course the first thing out of your mouth when you wake up is a complaint," I chided.

"So, did it work?" my sister asked, trying to brush off my comment.

"I don't know."

"What's my name?"

"Tiffany?" My sister frowned, disappointed. "I'm just kidding! I know it's Courtney!" He turned to me. "See, you're not the only one with jokes." Yeah, Robert, you should try stand-up.

"So it worked then?!" Courtney exclaimed. I felt like she was a bit overexcited for meeting someone for the first time consciously.

"I think so."

Courtney turned to me. "Matt, would you mind giving me a moment alone with Robert?"

Robert's face was puzzled. "Matt? Who the hell is Matt? Maybe the damn machine didn't work. Figures. Probably shoddy specs."

Courtney was equally puzzled. "That's my brother's name. You spent almost a month with him. How could you not have learned his name in all that time?"

"I think I might be able to explain." I interjected. "I kinda changed my name. Everyone knows a douchebag named Matt, so I had to change it. I go by Julian now."

Courtney didn't even try to make sense of it. "Well, Matt or Julian or whatever it is you'd like me to call you, could you give us a minute alone now?"

I couldn't agree fast enough. I was ready to get away from Robert as fast possible. If all went well, that would be the last interaction I ever had with the man. But Lady Luck wasn't particularly interested in acting like a lady. That bitch didn't even let me lube up before she fucked me again.

I walked down the hall and found a seat at a table. As I waited, no less than five smoking hot nurses passed by. If I wasn't waiting for my sister, I would have been all over them. I looked down at my watch. It had already been two minutes. I figured I would give her two more. That seemed like a fair trade, considering she only asked for one minute. After that, I was going chasing.

Alas, she walked down the hallway as I was in the last ten seconds of my countdown.

"What are you so happy about?" I asked. She was positively giddy.

"Oh, nothing," she said, trying to play coy like an innocent teenager. "Just that Robert asked me out."

Defeated, I put my head in my hands. I was never going to get rid of him. With my luck, Robert would end up marrying Courtney and I'd be stuck with him for good.

I walked my sister to her new apartment and gave her a kiss on the cheek. I'd gotten her a place just a couple blocks from my building so that I could keep a better eye on her.

It was almost midnight by the time I dropped my sister off, but my night was far from over. I still had some unfinished business to attend to. I couldn't let Robert end up with my sister. He was erratic, impulsive, and obnoxious at best; a cold blooded killer at worst. I couldn't let my sister see who he really was, not after everything she'd been through.

I walked back through the doors of the hospital and made a beeline for Robert's room. Naturally, the place was swarming with attractive nurses, all of whom seemed to be looking for a little bit of late night entertainment. Of course that would happen when I have a fucking agenda.

I passed by the nurses without so much as a glance, kicking myself in the ass the whole way, and walked into

Robert's room. He was sleeping peacefully. I pulled the chair out of the corner, slid it next to his bed, and kicked my feet up, thinking that I might wake him. I forgot how heavy a sleeper he was. I kicked him a few times in the side before clipping the IV in right hand, causing it to shift in his vein. Robert woke with a start.

"Julian? What are you doing back here?" he asked, groggily.

I rose from my chair and glared at Robert. "Stay away from my sister."

"What? What are you talking about?" He rubbed his eyes and sat up.

"I said stay away from my sister."

"I don't understand?" What, did I have to spell it out for him? I thought the stupid comments would have stopped when he got his memory back, but he must have always been a dumbass.

"You're not going anywhere near my sister. I don't want her around you. Not after everything she went through."

"Why? Julian, your sister is a grown woman. She can make her own decisions. She can decide who she sees and who she doesn't."

"Why? Why?!" I couldn't stand still. My blood was boiling. I paced around Robert's bed as I laid into him. "Are you fucking serious? Why? Robert, you're a psychopath. You're a fucking psychopath. I've watched you kill five people in the last two days. I watched you ruthlessly torment an innocent man without feeling a bit of remorse. Don't even fucking think about going near my sister or I will finish the job I started sixteen years ago."

Robert remained surprisingly calm. He looked nothing like the man I'd begrudgingly gotten to know over the past few weeks. His eyes had an inviting kindness to them. And when he spoke again, it was in a soft, gentle tone, not the abrasive anger that I was accustomed to. "I know you read through my journal. And you were right about a lot of that. But there's so much more that you don't know."

My rage still had not subsided and I continued to pace. "I don't care how much more there is to know. What could possibly justify everything I've seen you do?"

Robert looked at me and took a deep breath. "Let me start from the beginning..."